METHODS OF THE MASTERS

Monet

METHODS OF THE MASTERS

Monet

BERNARD MYERS

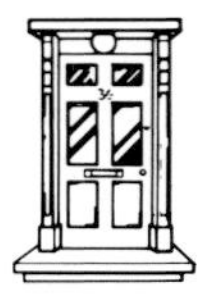

Brian Trodd Publishing House Limited

Published in 1990 by
Brian Trodd Publishing House Limited
27 Swinton Street, London WC1X 9NW

ISBN 1 85361 100 X

Printed in Hong Kong

Contents

What is Impressionism?

Claude Monet was an Impressionist, and his name has become almost synonymous with that artistic movement. In fact, Monet was inadvertently the means by which Impressionism got its name. In 1874, at the first exhibition by a loose co-operative of artists, all of whom were finding difficulty in showing and selling their work through the conventional salons and dealers, Monet exhibited a painting which he named *'The Port of Le Havre'*, and which he subtitled by way of further explanation *'Impression: Sunrise'*. The subtitle was seized upon by critics and journalists who, faced with describing unfamiliar paintings to the public, found it a very convenient way of conveying the intangible qualities of a very heterogeneous collection of new works. The word was used equally as a term of abuse and as a simple collective description.

That it ever was a term of abuse may puzzle subsequent generations. The works of the Impressionists must be among the most popular, the most accessible paintings ever produced. Their influence on the work of professionals and amateurs alike was and is universal. Reproductions hang in homes and hospitals, and their images adorn calendars and curtains, biscuit tins and chocolate boxes galore. Reproductions of works once decried as being by lunatics, incompetents, charlatans and mountebanks – and even called obscene – now hang in school classrooms everywhere and are taken for granted by children, for whom these are often the first works by professional artists to which they are introduced.

Impression: Soleil levant (Le Port du Havre par la brume)
1872 (dated 1873) Oil on canvas
48 x 63 cm (19 x 24 3/8 in)
Musée Marmottan, Paris
The sub-title of this painting, Impression: Sunrise, *gave the Impressionists their nickname. It seems remarkable that anyone could ever have been baffled by the pearly tints and brilliant brushwork of this picture. It is now missing from the museum.*

Claude Monet
1880

Individual paintings by these artists did challenge the social, moral and aesthetic conventions of their time, but such works were conspicuously few and far between. Far from deliberately courting notoriety or making overtly provocative statements, most Impressionist pictures are innocuous landscapes, portrayals of everyday middle-class life and simple still-life compositions of fruit or flowers. However these were as much the targets for the critics' anger, scorn and mockery as the occasional scenes from Bohemian low life.

Such attacks – easily taken up by the unthinking public, and by artists who were worried about upsetting the status quo and, in any case, rarely had actually seen the works for themselves – caused the Impressionists much bitterness and very real financial hardship. This bitterness was not always alleviated by the fact that these works did become accepted and popular in the lifetimes of most of their creators. Monet, in particular, lived to reap the fruits of a harvest sown with much pain in his early years; the memory of this clouded the years of prosperity of his old age.

The story is simple enough. A group of painters – rejected by the Salon (the virtually state-controlled annual exhibition which gave the stamp of approval to artists by showing their work), and shunned by the dealers upon whom the artists depended – decided to form a co-operative exhibiting society to show and market their own works. The well-known Parisian photographer Nadar was changing premises, and offered them, free of charge, the use of his studio in the Boulevard des Capucines in a fashionable quarter of Paris. The exhibition opened on 15 April 1874 and ran for one month. By 15 May, history had been made.

The exhibitors were optimistic. Camille Pissarro, sponsored by the aged Corot, had had paintings shown in the Salon which had garnered good reviews. He had also started to sell, as had Monet and Degas, who with Renoir were the four organizers of the 'Société Anonyme [limited company] of Painters, Sculptors and Engravers'. If only they could get a fair showing, they reasoned, and the public could see their work, they would be assured of success. The hostile reception was quite unexpected.

Manet, whose *Déjeuner sur l'herbe* and *Olympia* had caused such scandal when shown in, respectively, 1863 and 1865, had refused to be associated with the co-operative or exhibit with them. High-brow critics writing for the few were appreciative and understanding, but the middle-brow popular press treated the whole thing as an outrage or, even worse, a joke. And it was just to such readers that the Impressionists hoped to sell their work if only they could get them to see it: decorative pictures of popular subjects at modest prices; paintings to be hung in the home, not in grand salons; pictures that were private and intimate. Any would-be patrons who might have taken a chance now faced ridicule from their friends.

The affair became a matter of politics – an ideological, not an aesthetic issue. Those who defended the Impressionists were generally left wing and intellectual, while those who attacked them were right wing and populist. When the public heard the Impressionists being defended

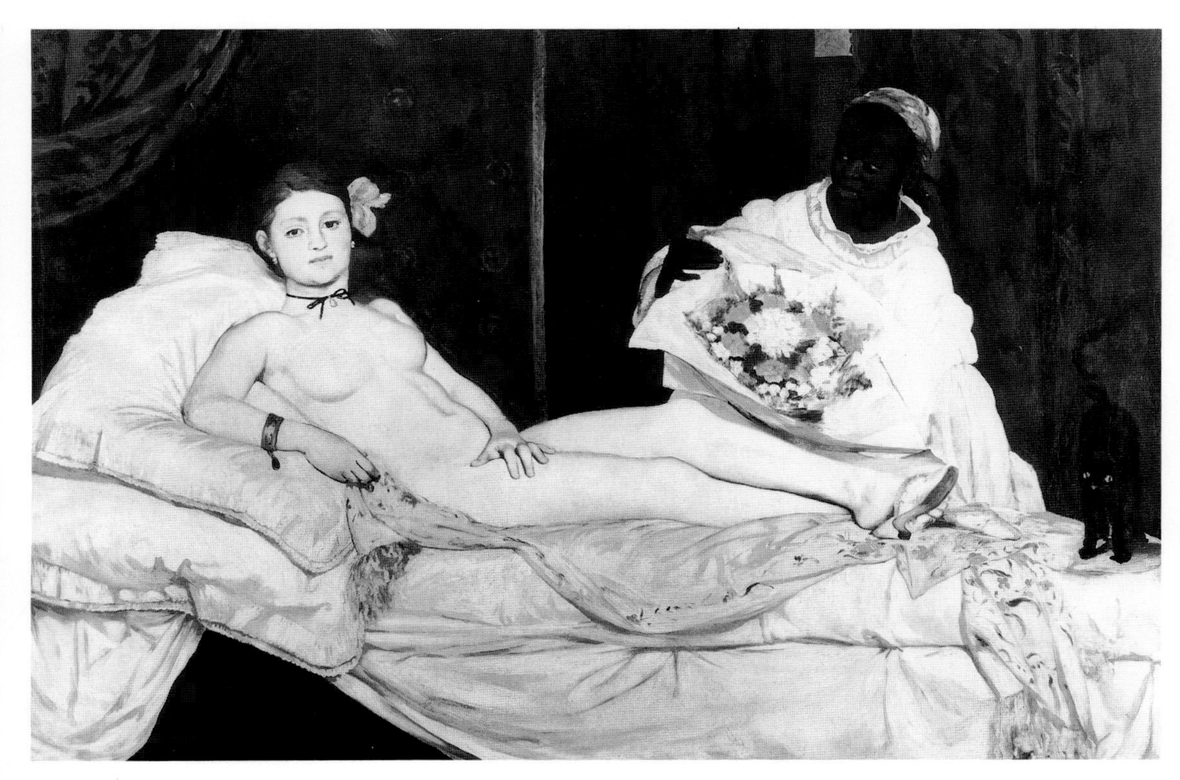

Left: Edouard Manet. *Olympia*
1863 Oil on canvas
130 × 190 cm (51 1/5 × 74 4/5 in)
Musée d'Orsay, Paris
A pictorial scandal. The nude model is no idealized Venus or Diana but a portrait of the notorious Victorine Meurend, who with a black beribboned neck gazes somewhat defiantly out of the picture. To make matters worse she is wearing high-heeled slippers.

Opposite: *Vase of Chrysanthemums*
1880 Oil on canvas
99.6 × 73 cm (39 1/4 × 28 3/4 in)
National Gallery of Art, Washington D.C. Chester Dale Collection
Between 1878 and 1882 Monet painted some 20 still life and flower pieces. Chrysanthemums were very much part of the vogue for things Japanese in Paris, and were a symbol of luxury and exoticism in the works of poets and novelists.

as realists, it was not the gentle Corot, a bachelor recluse living only to paint, who came to mind but the fiery Courbet, who was held personally responsible for the destruction of the Vendôme column during the Paris Commune of 1871. For the most part, however, these new painters wanted to live quiet lives in moderate comfort earning their living by painting.

Why, then, it must be asked, was this small group of struggling artists, with little in common beyond their poverty and not united by any programme or manifesto, branded as a band of dangerous lunatics? One answer can be found in the nature of the press itself. This depended on a new, large, newspaper-reading public that was essentially urban and largely metropolitan. Newspapers competed for readers, their owners for power and prestige, their political parties for votes, and their journalists for all that being a 'name' would give them in society. News tended to be sensationalized. Writers were extreme in their views and violent in their language, and this quite often spilled over into physical violence. Journalists and editors

fought duels, engaged in fisticuffs with readers, and were shot at by their victims. By and large, the true Bohemians were not art students but men of letters competing for patronage and attention in newspapers, journals and the theatre. The artists that they attacked or supported were, by association, tarred with the same brush.

Radical writers claimed to be realists, but this must be qualified. Their realism might lead them to employ working-class settings, characters and everyday speech, but their plots were pure melodrama with a content of crime and violence that was meant to shock. When the Impressionists spoke of their own realism, however, they meant not only their inclusion of subjects from everyday life but also the qualities of form, colour, light and air. Assuming that the word 'realism' had social and political overtones, writers and their readers looked for hidden meanings and motives in Impressionist painting, giving the work the literary content that they expected all art to have.

Patronage had changed, too. The descendants of the aristocratic survivors of the Revolution clung to the surroundings and art of the past. The new patrons were businessmen who were buying for the first time. Their tastes were as pragmatic as the conduct of their affairs. They were simple idealists in that they expected art to be above the mundane, everyday world, portraying virtues to which they paid lip service but did not practise. Art should be uplifting, beautiful in style, morally edifying in content, and didactic in the easily understood manner of popular proverbs. Its qualities should stand for permanence, static and unchanging in a world that was subject to change, decline and decay. They measured value with

Opposite top: *Destruction of the Vendôme Column*
1871 Engraving
This incident coupled revolutionary violence and modern art in the public eye.

Opposite left: *Poppies*
1875 Oil on canvas
50 × 65 cm (19 3/5 × 25 3/5 in)
Musée d'Orsay, Paris
A pastoral scene painted of and for townspeople.

Above: *Tulip Fields at Sassenheim*
1886 Oil on canvas
59.7 × 73.2 cm (23 1/2 × 28 4/5 in)
Sterling and Francine Clark Art Institute, Williamstown, Massachusetts
When Monet revisited earlier haunts he seemed to partly revert to earlier styles: particular places, for Monet, called for a particular painting response.

money, and paid *pro rata* for skill of execution and finish to a high standard. They loved attention to detail, pictures that could be easily read, which would be admired by like-minded friends and bring credit to the owner.

The Impressionists broke all these rules. Their landscapes included railway bridges and factory chimneys. They painted people in simple scenes from everyday life. Their subjects listened to bands in the park, danced in tavern gardens and dance halls, went to cafés for a drink, or to the circus, the music hall, the races. They painted popular singers in cabaret acts, and ballet dancers waiting in the wings. They painted people at work, paviours digging up streets, railwaymen in the yards, laundresses ironing, shop girls at the milliner's, waitresses serving blue-smocked porters.

Impressionism was essentially an urban movement. The painters saw even the countryside through townsmen's eyes. They centred on Paris rather than the provinces, living and working in the suburbs, commuting by train. Their pastoral scenes are of townspeople spending a day in the country, walking through fields in their Sunday best and carrying parasols, boating on the river Seine, dancing at country inns.

The Impressionists painted what pleased them, and painted how they pleased. A picture was finished when the painter declared it so, not when it had been worked up to an acceptable laid-down standard. In short, they painted to please themselves, not the critics, not the Salon, not the dealers, not the public.

At best, this appeared to be pure self-indugence, at worst an insulting gesture to critics and public, flouting all the rules of taste and art, which could only lead, if taken to its conclusion, to a breakdown in the standards of conventional behaviour and an undermining of society. The public naturally assumed that artists who were so completely self-indulgent in their work would be equally so in matters of financial honesty, sexual morality, care of family, regard for property and respect for authority. Unable to see its favourite virtues in Impressionism, society saw its favourite vices instead.

The Impressionists may not have been consciously advocating social change, but they

The Picnic
1873 – 74 Oil on canvas
160 x 201 cm (63 x 79 1/8 in)
Musée d'Orsay, Paris
Painted in his garden at Argenteuil, the crumpled napkin and nearly empty wine glasses show that the open air luncheon is over.

Monet's son Jean plays with his bricks while his mother, Camille, walks along the well-kept path with a visitor. A beribboned straw hat hangs in the tree, and her parasol and large purse lie on the bench.

certainly reflected it. In the time of a single lifespan, from 1789, the French had experienced revolution, counter-revolution, imperialism, dictatorship, war and civil war. The nation was a byword for political instability, and the populace had had more than enough of upheaval.

There was also technological change, and this had a deep if not always overt effect upon Impressionism. With the technical revolution in materials, painters were freed from the labour of grinding dry pigment into mixtures of oils and solvents, necessitating a workshop and studio pupil-assistants. Artists could now buy paints ready mixed in collapsible metal tubes which would keep without drying out and could be carried in a box, ready for use, to the chosen site, along with a portable easel and prepared canvases or boards. They could be out, work on the spot and be back at the studio on the same day – and this was made even easier by the development of the railways.

New colours were created, of great brightness and intensity, the fruits of industrial chemistry and the modern dye-stuffs industry. The Impressionist's bible of colour theory – *The Laws of Contrast of Colour and Their Application to the Arts* (generally abbreviated to *On Colour*) – was the work of M. E. Chevreul. Chevreul was not an artist, designer or aesthete but an industrial chemist and civil servant. The French government having set him the task of developing a synthetic butter substitute, he christened his successful product 'margarine' – literally 'pearl-like'. He was then sent to sort out a problem at the state-owned Gobelin dye and tapestry works.

Established in 1662, over two centuries of tapestry production there, largely based on literal copies of paintings or painters' designs, had resulted in a legacy of thousands of tints and shades of dyed yarns – and in wasteful confusion. Chevreul was

Diagram. *It was the scientist Chevreul who taught painters and designers about the optical mixing of solid colour. In this diagram the blue, yellow and orange-red patches are very much 'reduced' dull colours on their own: in the lower half these identical colours are mixed in spots and become brilliant touches of colour, ranging from green to orange and yellow. This is the heart of Impressionist technique.*

Opposite: *Photograph of Chevreul and Nadar* 1886
On the eve of the scientist Eugene Chevreul's 101st birthday, the photographer Nadar (Gaspard Félix Tournachon) interviewed him in an early essay in photo-journalism. A series of photographs was taken by an assistant during a dialogue between the men who, in different ways, were strong outside influences on the Impressionist painters. A colour wheel used by Chevreul to demonstrate his theory of colour mixing is conspicuous in the photograph.

Left: *Rouen Cathedral. Main Door. Harmony in White*
1894 Oil on canvas
106 x 75 cm (41¾ x 29½ in)
Musée d'Orsay, Paris
Monet always denied that he painted from photographs. A suggestion that he may have done so was the cause of a final quarrel between himself and the painter Sargent. What is beyond doubt is that his vision was influenced by photography. In spite of the restricted site in front of the façade of Rouen Cathedral, Monet did not have to cut off his angle of view in this way. Painters were used to reassembling their sketches from awkward angles into complete views in their studios. That this view of Rouen was acceptable to the painter and his public was due to the fact that they had been 'taught' by photography.

to impose some sort of order and classification on this proliferation, and to effect economies in production. He observed and carefully recorded the mutual effect of colours and tones in juxtaposition, and recommended mixing and matching colours by spinning coloured yarns together – for example, forming green from quantities of yellow and blue threads – rather than dyeing new batches every time a change of colour was needed. He quantified colour mixtures by use of a colour wheel, whose measurable segments of colour 'mixed' optically when the wheel was spun.

Chevreul's *On Colour*, his summation of his work at the Gobelin works and first published in 1839, ran into many editions and printings and was widely translated. Its illustrations were printed using the technique of colour chromolithography, which meant that the mutual effect of colours that he discussed in highly technical language could be seen by readers themselves, and not have to be imagined or reconstructed by students as in all previous treatises on colour. The work was seized on by dye-stuff and textile manufacturers who were experiencing difficulty in matching dye batches in mass production, by architects and interior designers, by textile and wallpaper designers and, with unexpected enthusiasm, by the 'fine' artists.

Much has also been made of the influence on Impressionism of the then recent invention of photography. There had been wild speculation that photography would make painting obsolete, but in fact, the reverse happened: photography gave painting new stimulus and freedom. First and foremost, it taught artists to see, freed from the conventions of drawing that had accumulated

Diagram. *This diagrammatic sketch shows the traditional method of underpainting for a figure, either for a classical 'history' painting or for a portrait. The painting is quite transparent, but exaggeratedly dark. All compositional details would be settled at this stage.*

Diagram. *The next stage in a figure painting or portrait would be to paint in the warm flesh tone. This layer of paint is mixed with white and is therefore opaque, but it is thinly spread out over the shadows. These turn blue or cold, not through the addition of colour but optically, the finished painting varying in thickness from light to shadow.*

through practice and turned into cliché. Photography arrested birds in flight and animals in motion. Its black-and-white nature helped painters to observe and render tone by recording light and shade divorced from local colour. It gave them referential material for landscape, townscape and architecture. But the main influence was in the very limitations of photography. Its flat, one-eyed view of limited boundaries, which simplified receding planes and 'cut off' the scene and framed it arbitrarily, taught the Impressionists how to compose and maintain an effect of spontaneity, the snap-shot or *coup d'oeil* as opposed to the formalized static arrangement of figures or objects in space.

The technical revolution in painting itself lay at the heart of Impressionism and is essential to the understanding of what is meant by Impressionism and painting since Impressionism. The traditional method of painting which Impressionism

Diagram. *By contrast, a portrait by Manet, or Monet, or late 19th-century portrait painters would be blocked in in tones matching the warm and cold tones of the sitter's head. The drawing would be in brown, grey or blue, and the underpainting grey or blue. Gradually the portrait would be corrected and refined in detail. Right from the beginning the paint is evenly thick all over, and would increase in thickness as the painting draws to a finish.*

replaced was 300 years old. Innovatory in its time, it had become the most general technique of the 'Masters' and their followers, largely superseding the older methods of fresco painting, encaustic painting in wax, and painting in distemper and tempera, all of which became limited to particular usage by decorators and illustrators.

Long before the nature of light had become the object of measurement and scientific observation, it was a matter of common observation that there is a visual difference between what might be called 'reflected' and 'transmitted' light. If we look at the rising smoke of a bonfire against a dark background of trees, the vapour appears as a blue mist. If we look at at the same smoke against the light – against, for example, a bright cloud or the sun – it appears to be a ruddy orange-brown. Against the dark background, we are looking at light reflected from the smoke, while against the sun we are looking at light being transmitted through it.

The smoke itself consists of minute particles of matter, drops of moisture and light carbon ash which act as filters. The particles are fine enough to scatter the shorter wave-lengths of light, the blue end of the spectrum, but allow through the longer wave-lengths, the red end of the spectrum. Leonardo da Vinci is credited with the first observed account of this phenomenon and its use in painting.

We are really looking at particles suspended in a fluid medium – smoke in air. We can see this clearly in a glass of soapy water: blue with the light, red against it. Rogue milkmen who watered the milk were said to turn it blue. This phenomenon is everywhere in nature. The same scattering of light gives us our blue sky. The brilliant blue of the wings of the tropical butterflies of the *Morphoidae* family is just such an optical blue: the minute ridges and scales on the wings scatter and reflect blue light, while the longer wave-lengths pass through and are absorbed by the brown membrane, as we can see if we hold the insect against the light. The same effect is seen in peacocks' tail feathers, on beetles's backs, and on certain cloudy gemstones such as opals.

This was at the heart of the so-called 'secret' techniques of the Old Masters. Imagine that we are watching a portrait being painted. The artist carefully draws the head on a prepared board or canvas. Then in red-brown paint he 'blocks' in the solid form of the features, quite simply and broadly but with care, and exaggerating the depth and extent of the brown shadows. This layer of paint will be transparent, rather thin and diluted. The artist wants it to dry quickly and dry hard, so that he can get on with the next stage without disturbing it. Most masters had their own formulae for achieving this with various mixtures of oils and solvents.

The painter now mixes a range of flesh tones on his palette. These will be warm, rose-pink to brown-yellow as required, and quite dense, with plenty of white pigment in the mixtures. He then works from the light areas of his portrait to the dark. In the light areas, he puts on the densest paint, but thins it out as he works into the shadow, not diluting his paint with solvent but physically

Above: Rembrandt Van Rijn.
A Woman Bathing in a Stream
1654 Oil on panel
61.8 × 47 cm (24³/8 × 18¹/2 in)
National Gallery, London

Even a black and white photograph clearly shows the varying thickness of paint, with its opacity, translucency, and transparency.

stretching it out into the thinnest of layers until it virtually disappears. As the pink flesh tints are smeared over the red-brown ground, they turn blue, like the soapy water or thinned milk.

When this stage of the painting is completed to the artist's satisfaction, he puts in the highlights and details, redrawing as required: the final and all-important top layer, the *finish*. He has now achieved not only a recognizable likeness through his skill in drawing but an approximation to nature. The layers of paint pass imperceptibly from cold highlight to warm flesh, from cold, bluish half-tone in which we can imagine that we see the blood beneath the skin, to the dark, warm, light-absorbing shadow implying absence of light. A touch of carmine red in the corner of the eye or the shading of a nostril or the lobe of an ear enhance the illusion that we are looking not at paint but at flesh and blood. Not only portraits of living personages but the mythical gods and goddesses themselves came to life via this technique. In the hands of a master, it was a sure foundation upon which he built his own artistic personality, as particular and as dissimilar as, say, Rembrandt is from Rubens.

The technique seems, and was, very simple, but it had its disadvantages. It allowed for little or no overworking. Artists could not change their minds or their drawings without virtually starting again – overworking killed the life in a painting. It called for great skill in drawing and a strict discipline in technique. However, it enabled the fullest use of the limited range of pigments available at the time. Dull earth colours became

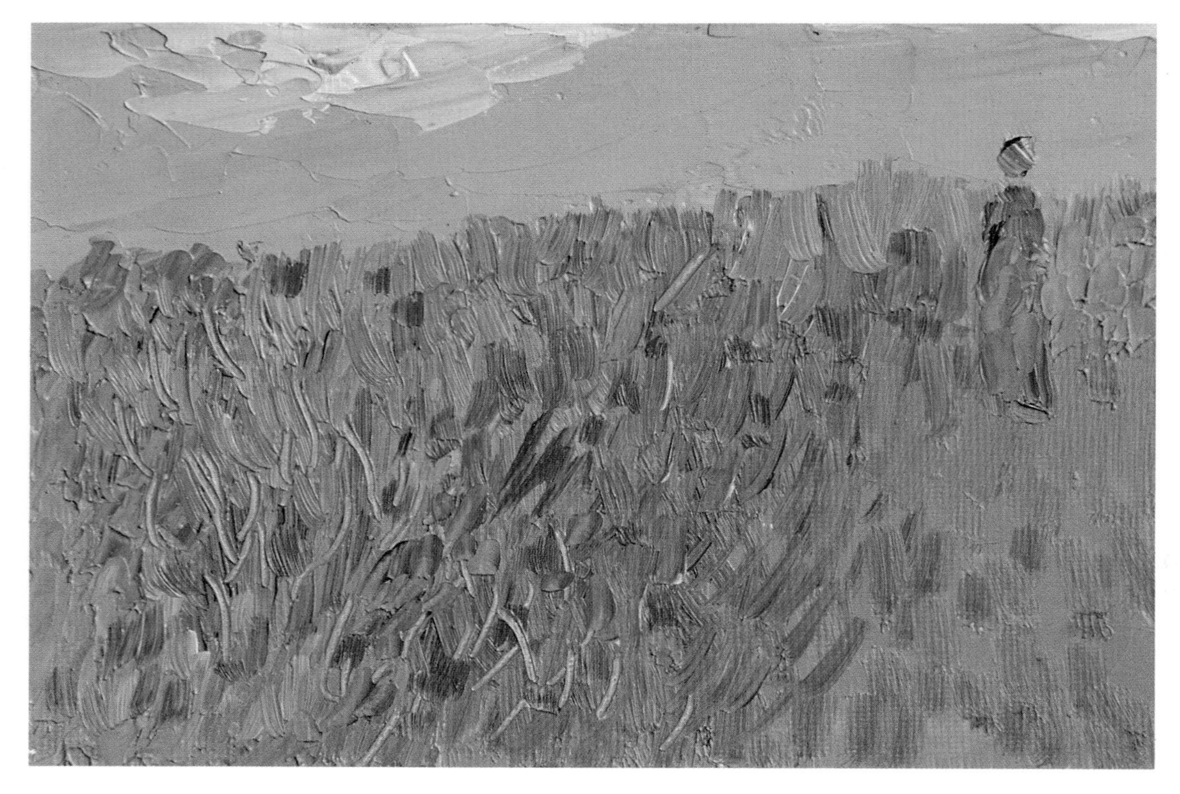

Opposite top: *Banks of the Seine, Vétheuil*
1880 Oil on canvas
73.4 × 100.5 cm (28⁷/8 × 39¹/2 in)
National Gallery of Art, Washington D.C. Chester Dale Collection
Here Monet demonstrates his vocabulary of brushwork, matching the scale and rhythm of the touches of paint to clouds, trees, sky, water, and the intricacies and variety of grasses and wild flowers.

Left: Diagram. *In all Monet's painting it is the final surface that expresses the image. Here in this diagram we have a much simplified system. From right to left is a grey-green tonal ground, with suggestions of broken colour in blue shadow, then strokes suggesting leaves and flowers, and then the bright yellow-green lights added. The master work would be built up of innumerable fine touches.*

brilliant in juxtaposition. Splendid blues were obtained from simple mixtures of black and white, greens from black and yellow. The paint remained luminous, clear. Landscape and marine painters, in particular, made full use of the technique, especially in their skies: the red ground peeping through green foliage enhanced the greenness and gave mysterious depth to a clump of trees; distant hills echoed the blueness of nature by the same means.

This was the technique used by painters as late as Turner and Constable, immediate predecessors to the Impressionists. However, despite all their working from nature, the free handling of their paint and brushes, their capturing the impression of the moment of sunrise or sunset, they were not proto-Impressionists. Nor were their immediate predecessors in France, the realists such as Courbet and the out-of-door painters of the Barbizon school.

The Impressionists were not ignorant of this tradition. No painter who had seriously studied at the Louvre could be. It was not merely a cliché in the hands of the Salon painters who they despised, but it had been used by painters whom they idolized: Courbet and Delacroix. They even practised it themselves, on occasion, particularly Renoir and Degas, and Monet himself. But generally it was not relevant to their aims in painting, and they had to find an alternative technique to carry out these aims.

The technique had to reflect spontaneity of observation and an immediate directness of execution matched to an immediacy of vision. Their technique evolved from painting directly on the spot, trying to equate paint on canvas with what they saw in nature, matching tone for tone, change with change, obliterating the tentative first essay, not preserving it, constantly altering and repainting on the same canvas, adjusting passage to passage until they arrived, not at that *finish* of the Masters, but at the last spontaneous touch – even if it was added much later, back at the studio. It was that final touch that counted.

Thaw on the Seine near Bennecourt
1893 Oil on canvas
65 × 100 cm ($25^{3}/_{5}$ × $39^{2}/_{5}$ in)
Walker Art Gallery, Liverpool
One of a series of paintings of ice floes on the Seine as the river thaws. The first were made in the winter of 1880 at Vétheuil, which was particularly severe, and then Monet returned to the subject after his move to Giverny. The paintings were started on the spot. Monet must have worked fast, what with the cold, the short day, and the rapidly changing scene, and then finished the pictures in the studio without destroying their spontaneity.

The Early Years

Claude Monet was born in Paris on 14 November 1840, the son of a wholesale provision merchant. The family moved to the Channel port of Le Havre at the mouth of the river Seine when Monet was five years old. From that time, the painter's life was to be divided between Paris and Le Havre, and when he finally settled down, it was at Giverny on the Seine between the two.

In 1900, at the age of 60, Monet gave an interview to the Paris newspaper *Le Temps*, in which he talked about his childhood. He described himself as a strong, vigorous boy who hated school, was not fond of parental discipline and ran wild. His two loves were the sea and drawing. He filled his school books with caricatures of his teachers and, by the age of 15, was executing commissions at 20 francs per portrait. Surviving examples show a slick competence in the genre of the time. The local frame-maker placed examples of Monet's work in his shop window, and the boy, full of self-importance, hung about the pavement to catch people's remarks as they recognized one another. Monet boasted that he could have become a millionaire if he had 'kept along those lines', but his restlessness and curiosity intervened.

Some small beach scenes also displayed in the frame-maker's window attracted his scorn. Monet

Right: Eugène Boudin *Trouville*
1897 Oil on canvas
36 x 58.5 cm (14 1/5 x 23 in)
Richard Green, London
Boudin quietly painted away on the Norman coast, where he evolved a personal style full of bright light and sea breezes. Few of his paintings are of fisherfolk and their boats, but of fashionably dressed Parisians taking the sea air. Seaside holidays were made fashionable by the Empress Eugénie and her court.

Left: *Caricature of Mario Ochard*
1856 – 58 Graphite pencil on paper
31.8 x 24.6 cm (12 1/2 x 9 1/2 in)
Art Institute of Chicago.
Gift of Mr. and Mrs. Carter H. Harrison
This drawing, said to be of Monet's art master, is a typical example of the caricatures that the 18-year-old 'Oscar' Monet, as he was known at the time, showed in the picture framer's shop window to the astonishment, he claimed, of passers by in Le Havre.

set great store by technical skill, and these works appeared to him to be slight and sketchy, lacking the style and slick finish to which he aspired. Monet wondered how the artist could have the nerve to sign and exhibit them, but the frame-maker chided him for his ignorance. 'You ought to get to know Monsieur Boudin,' he advised the young man. 'He has studied in Paris and could teach you a thing or two.'

Eugène Boudin (1824–98) was born at Honfleur on the Seine estuary opposite Le Havre, the son of a coastal pilot. Originally, he had been a frame-maker, painting when he could, but was encouraged by his customers to sell his shop to Monet's new patron and paint full-time. He spent his working life on the Normandy coast, painting seascapes and beach and harbour scenes in which ladies wear crinolines and gentlemen silk top hats as beach wear. He painted in the open air on the spot, and luminous skies only to be found at the ocean's edge dominated his pictures.

He advised Monet to follow his example, which the boy found extraordinary. However, his curiosity aroused, the young artist eventually succumbed and became Boudin's pupil. He announced to his family that he was going to be a painter and wished to go to Paris. According to Monet, the family, led by his father, was totally opposed. However, he had saved all his money earned from caricatures, and 'aged 16, when one feels rich with 2000 francs in one's pocket, I set out for Paris.' For all Monet's bravado, the facts were not quite like this. He had been encouraged by an aunt who painted and was a knowledgeable collector, and his father had tried to obtain a municipal grant for his son to study in Paris, with Boudin named as his teacher. Later, it was his aunt who would pay for his return to Paris in 1862. His family were far more worried about his youth and wildness than about his decision to become a painter and, as it turned out, with good reason.

His parents hoped that, once in Paris, Monet would enrol in a serious *atelier* where he would practise drawing and pursue a laborious course of studies, but he proved to be as wild in the capital as he had been in Le Havre. He was given an introduction to Constant Troyon (1810–65), painter in the Flemish landscape tradition, but Monet thought him a bore. Instead he joined the Académie Suisse, a misnomer for a dilapidated shed of a workshop managed by a superannuated male artist's model named Suisse.

Those who used this *atelier* worked or not as they thought fit, indulged in violent horse-play and struggled to become painters free from the prevailing Academic styles. Monet later was to confess to Courbet, to whom he was introduced at the Brasserie Martyrs, that he led a dissipated life and wasted a good deal of his time.

This conventionally Bohemian lifestyle was

abruptly drawn to an end when Monet's number was drawn in the lottery and he was called up for military service. His parents, believing that the threat of a spell in the army would bring him to his senses, said that they would only buy him out on condition that he returned home. They were to be disappointed. Monet entered the army and thoroughly enjoyed the life, particularly his service in North Africa, which for him was an exotic

Below: *Windmill near Zaandam*
1871 Oil on canvas
43 x 73 cm ($16\frac{7}{8}$ x $28\frac{3}{4}$ in)
Ashmolean Museum, Oxford
In Holland after the Franco–Prussian war Monet painted rather sombre tonal pictures very much influenced by Jongkind.

Right: *Self portrait*
1886 Oil on canvas
56 x 46 cm (22 x $18\frac{1}{8}$ in)
Private collection

Below right: *Photograph of Claude Monet*
An interesting comparison with Monet's own self image.

Johan Barthold Jongkind.
Windmill near Water
1860 Oil on canvas
42 × 56.5 cm (16½ × 22¼ in)
Richard Green, London
Monet had met Jongkind at Le Havre in 1862. A freer and richer painter than Boudin, and altogether on a broader scale, Jongkind's example set the seal on the first stage of the young Monet's development, and influenced Monet's own response to the Dutch landscape some ten years later.

revelation of colour. After two years' service, he developed anaemia and was invalided out.

Back at Le Havre in the summer of 1862, Monet met the Dutch painter Johan Barthold Jongkind (1819–91) who was then painting along the Normandy coast. Jongkind completed the initiation that Boudin had begun. 'It was as if a veil had been torn from my eyes,' Monet wrote. '... I understood. I grasped what painting was capable of being.' Monet's aunt, Madame Lecadre, complained that her nephew now never finished his pictures but left them as rough drafts which he defiantly flaunted. 'He pays no attention to my remarks,' she complained.

In November 1862, however, she enabled him to return to Paris. For his part, Monet promised to study seriously at a reputable *atelier*. Through his aunt's influence, he enrolled as a student of

Right: Edouard Manet. *Concert in the Tuileries*
1862 Oil on canvas
76.2 x 118.1 cm (30 x 46½ in)
National Gallery, London
This informal arrangement of the crowd of listeners, apparently caught by the painter on the spur of the moment, was carefully assembled in the studio from photographs of the painter's friends and acquaintances with the setting made from sketches on the spot.

Below right: Edouard Manet. *Le déjeuner sur l'herbe*
1863 Oil on canvas
214 x 270 cm (84¼ x 106¼ in)
Musée d'Orsay, Paris
Shown at the Salon des Refusés, Napoléon III called the picture indecent. Although the theme was a common one in high renaissance paintings as concerts champêtre, *or* Judgement of Paris, *which exist in many versions, this juxtaposition of an unidealized naked portrait with men in everyday dress, was too much for respectable contemporary taste.*

Opposite top: *Le déjeuner sur l'herbe à Chailly*
1865–66 Oil on canvas
130 x 181 cm (51¼ x 73 in)
Pushkin Museum of Fine Arts, Moscow
In this sketch, inspired by Manet's picture, and in direct emulation, Monet determined to show how open-air painting should be done. Manet's Déjeuner *is obviously of models posed in a studio against a painted backdrop, resulting in a highly artificial picture. Monet worked from sketches and figure studies made on the spot. This sketch for the life size work shows what Monet intended but never completed.*

Charles Gleyre (1808–74), among whose pupils were Auguste Renoir (1841–1919), Alfred Sisley (1839–99) and Frédéric Bazille (1841–70), the son of a prosperous wine producer. Killed in the Franco-Prussian war, it is impossible to say how Bazille might have fulfilled himself as a painter, but he became Monet's closest friend and financial mainstay, saving him from homelessness and starvation during his most difficult years.

The year 1863 saw the first public exhibition by Edouard Manet (1832–83) at the Galerie Martinet. This included the portrait of Lola de Valence, which owed much to Velasquez, and, much more important to the younger painters, the *Concert in the Tuileries (Musique aux Tuileries)*. The poet Baudelaire, whose likeness is in the picture, wrote of the poetry of frock coats and top hats, making a direct comparison with the *fêtes galantes* of the 18th-century painters Watteau, Fragonard and Lancret, whose elegant persons in gorgeous clothes are seen listening to music in the open air. This translation of a past genre into modern times and modern dress was a constant practice of Manet's. Critics misinterpreted and misrepresented this as plagiarism, but the real truth is that Manet was as much fascinated by the world of art as by the real world.

The jury of the Salon of 1863 was exceptionally conservative, and the members were accused of using their monopoly to discourage competition. The press turned the issue into a political scandal, and it was brought to the attention of the Emperor Louis Napoleon (Napoleon III). The Emperor, who had broken the French constitution by proclaiming himself as such, thought that, by intervening in the dispute, he could show himself to be a popular democrat on an unimportant issue. Asking to be shown the rejected works, he pronounced them to be quite as good as those which had been accepted, and he ordered that they were to be shown in the Palais de l'Industrie as a *Salon des Refusés.* This never-to-be-repeated event was to have a marked influence on the development of French painting.

The centrepiece of the exhibition and the cause of a great scandal was another painting by Manet, *Le déjeuner sur l'herbe* (literally 'Luncheon on the grass' but usually translated as 'The Picnic'). The theme had passed through several hands before it was adopted and adapted by Manet.

Originally an idea of Giorgione, (*c.* 1476–1510), it was copied by Raphael and then engraved by Mercantio. The pairing of a clothed male and a nude female, with poetically erotic overtones, was a repeated theme of Giorgione, much repeated by others, but what was acceptable in the work of an Old Master was thought immodest by the Emperor and shocking by the critics and public. If 'realism' in art is somehow related to common experience, then Giorgione was no more painting an everyday event in his time than Manet in his. Realism, shocking and crude, was implied by the modern dress rather than by anything else in the picture, which is obviously a studio piece of awkwardly posed models against a background of painted stage scenery.

The *Déjeuner* is a sombre affair. The young man dressed as a student is holding forth to the bored young woman who is much more interested in us, the spectators. The lugubrious scene does not excite envy or make us wish that we were there, unlike Renoir's boating lunches. In the *Déjeuner*, as in his *Tuileries*, Manet revived traditional themes in French painting – music, food and drink in the open air, young people, sunlight, trees and water – and a cycle of such picnic scenes by other artists followed but, in these, gaiety and charm were restored.

If Manet's *Déjeuner* evoked a response in the young painters generally, it triggered off in Monet an apparent act of monumental folly. At that time, he appeared to be on the brink of some success. He had had two views of Honfleur accepted by the Salon and the critics had noticed them and praised them (although Manet was infuriated by their confusing Monet's name with his). In addition, Monet's family had at last begun to take him seriously as a painter. Encouraged by this turn of good fortune, he took himself off to the Forest of Fontainebleau in the footsteps of the Barbizon painters. However, unlike his forerunners who had painted small, portable easel pictures, Monet embarked upon a canvas of over 30 sq. m (323 sq. ft), larger than any of Courbet's paintings. He boarded at an inn at Chailly, and worked in a shed from sketches made in the open air on the spot. Monet's *Déjeuner sur l'herbe à Chailly*, inspired partly by that of Manet and the latter's *Tuileries*, was designed to show how it *should* be done, with real figures in a real landscape, with some dozen people in suits and crinolines picnicking in a sunlit glade in the woods. He worked for months on this giant, unsaleable, perhaps unfinishable picture, work that consumed time, materials, energy and money. In the end, he had to leave the painting with the innkeeper as a surety against unpaid board and lodging. Later Monet retrieved the canvas which had been rolled up and stored in a cellar, but it had been ruined by damp, so he cut it up (fragments form a special exhibit in the Musée d'Orsay).

Monet should have been discouraged. Instead, he embarked on another large canvas that came to be known as *Women in the Garden (Femmes au jardin)*, painted in 1866–67. Not as large as his abortive *Déjeuner*, which had been too big to be painted out of doors, this canvas measures 265 × 208cm (104¼ × 81⅞ in), and Monet attempted to paint the whole composition in the open air. Working through the summer of 1866 at Ville d'Avray, he had a deep trench dug in the garden into which the canvas could be lowered by an arrangement of pulleys so that he could reach the top and the bottom equally easily. Courbet heard of this and disapproved, and Manet and Degas remarked that painting was too serious a matter to be treated as an outdoor sport. The painting was successfully completed, but then it was rejected by the Salon. They did, however, accept a life-size portrait of Monet's mistress Camille Doncieux, who had been the model for all three women on the left-hand side of the *Garden*.

Above: *Le déjeuner sur l'herb à Chailly*
1865–66 Oil on canvas
Centre fragment 248 × 217 cm (97³/₅ × 85²/₅ in)
Musée d'Orsay, Paris
Monet's would-be masterpiece was never finished. Monet had to abandon it to a creditor. When he eventually recovered it in 1884, large areas of it were irreparably damaged.

Opposite: *Bazille and Camille*
1865–66 Oil on canvas
93 × 69 cm (36³/₅ × 27¹/₅ in)
National Gallery of Art, Washington D.C. Ailsa Mellon Bruce Collection
A study painted on the spot for the Déjeuner. *Bazille also posed for the figure lying under the tree on the right, and Camille apparently posed for all the female figures.*

Claude Monet

Opposite: *Women in the Garden*
1866 – 67 Oil on canvas
265 x 208 cm (104¼ x 81⅞ in)
Musée d'Orsay, Paris
This large canvas was painted by Monet entirely in the open air. Although the painting was not made from photographs, the clear definition of light and strongly cast shadow with blocked-in tones, could well deceive one into thinking that it was.

Left: Edouard Manet. *Le bon bock*
1873 Oil on canvas
135.9 x 123.8 cm (53½ x 48¾ in)
Philadelphia Museum of Art, Pennsylvania. Mr. and Mrs. Carroll S. Tyson Collection
At various times Manet worked in the manner of Velasquez, Goya, and here, Frans Hals. The Café Guerbois in Montmartre was a favourite meeting place for painters where Manet held court. Here he sketched his friends, and painted the engraver Bellot enjoying a beer and a pipe. This painting in Flemish style was a popular exhibit at the Salon of 1873, and Manet was becoming a respectable figure.

Impressionist techniques

Women in the Garden, a landmark in Monet's work, is an excellent example of his technique at this time. Although it appears that he was trying to emulate the large-scale works of Courbet to win a reputation as the latter's successor, his technique is nothing like Courbet's. The older artist was still painting in the classical tradition. Although his brushwork was bold and vigorous, and he made emphatic use of the palette knife, Courbet's paint varies in thickness according to light and shade, with warm transparent shadows, dense opaque highlights and extensive use of scumbling, or dragged paint, and thin glazes. Monet, on the other hand, painted in thick, evenly applied paint, trying to match tones in solid blocks. The free touches and dabs of paint that he learned to use from Boudin to imply spontaneity and movement worked on an intimate scale, but would have been impossible in such a monumental work.

Manet had worked on this scale, but had taken the Spanish painters Goya and Velasquez, and even the Flemish painter Frans Hals, as his masters. Manet's painting is fluid, wet-looking, and the brush strokes blend. He was essentially a studio painter working from sketches. A dandy by nature, fastidious in his person and his dealings with others, conservative and aloof, Manet was concerned to achieve his effects *à la prima*, with a direct touch and as little overworking as possible, to keep his paintings fresh and to show off his skill.

In painting entirely in the open air, Monet set himself other problems. In later life, he was to claim that he personally discovered open-air painting – 'a dangerous innovation' he called it – and introduced his fellow students, Pissarro, Renoir and Sisley, to it. This is an exaggeration. After all, Boudin himself had introduced Monet

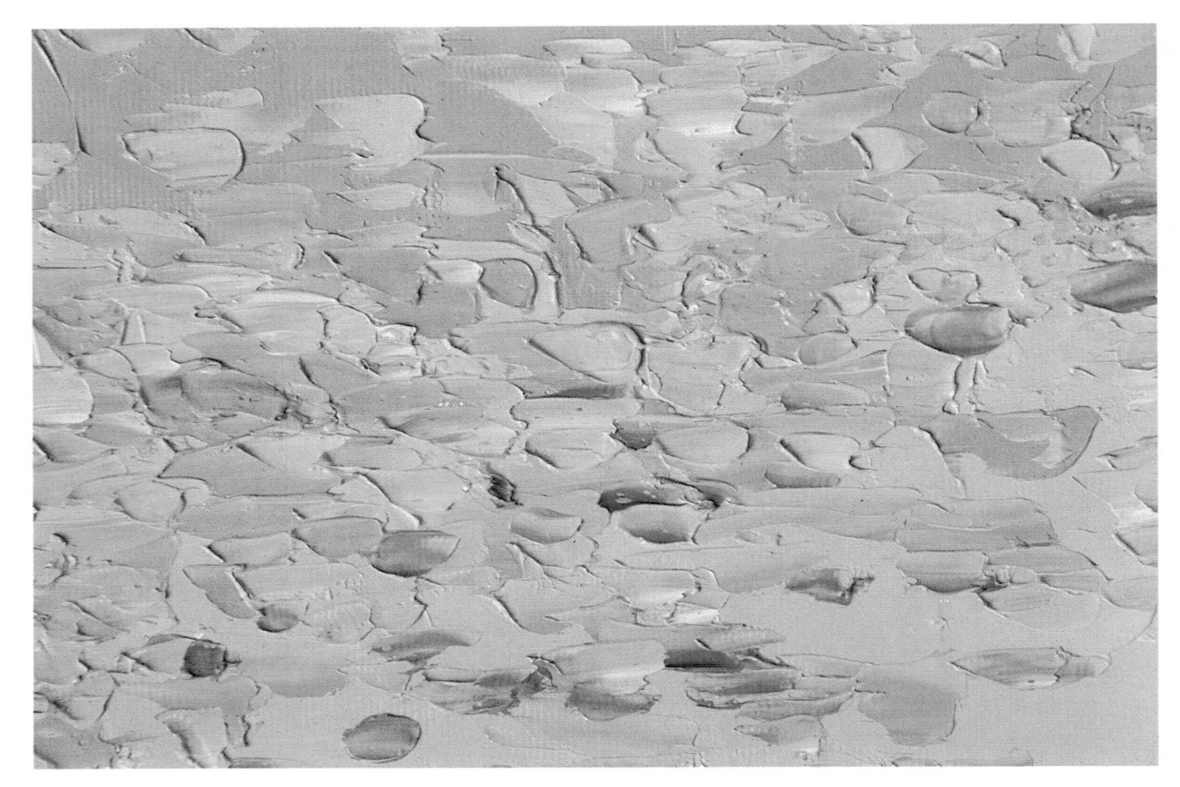

Right: Frédéric Bazille.
Family Reunion
1867 Oil on canvas
152 x 230 cm (59⅞ x 90½ in)
Musée d'Orsay, Paris
Contemporary with Monet's attempts to paint realistic groups in the open air, Bazille, who appears twice in the Déjeuner, *painted from photographs in the family album.*

Diagram. *Monet frequently used counterchange in his work. In this diagrammatic demonstration two tones of grey-brown and grey-green are laid in diagonally across the canvas. Then touches of grey-green are painted into the brown, and vice versa. Then light blue, dark blue and yellow are added to imply shadow and reflection on the surface of the water.*

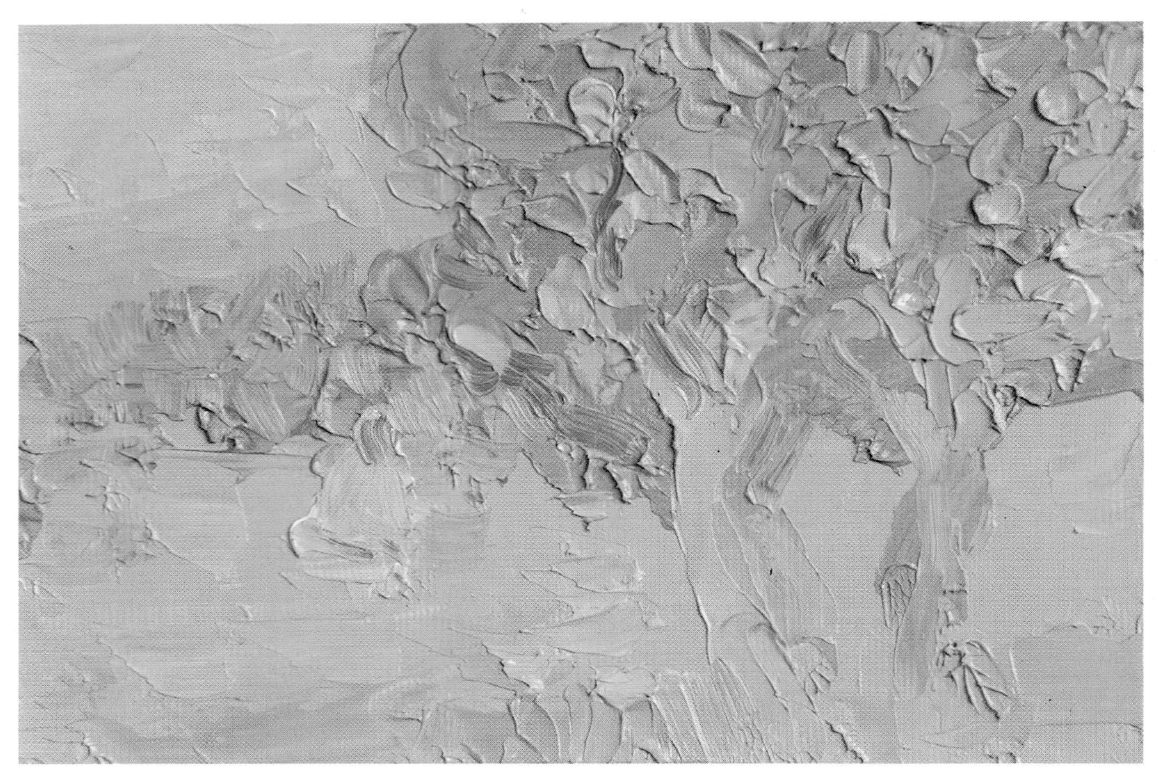

Diagram. *One would expect the background to be painted in first, and then the middle and foreground objects to be applied on top, such as figures and trees. Monet often blocked such objects in and then repainted the background colour, such as sky, on top once more, so that touches of sky blue are on top of the foliage of trees, as in this diagram.*

to *plein air* painting, very much against Monet's will at first, and Boudin had been preceded by the Barbizon painters who had made a virtue of the practice.

However, no one had attempted such a large-scale painting on the spot. Critics looked upon Boudin's work as studies or sketches, clever and charming in themselves but falling short of 'real' painting. Monet, too, had suffered criticism as a sketcher who never finished a picture. In this work, he set out to show that a large-scale painting could be finished on site. In doing so, he had to employ a technique quite unlike previous *plein air* painting.

The paint is applied in thick, dense patches – in effect, painting *on* painting rather than painting *into* painting. The *Women in the Garden* and Monet's *Déjeuner* are both careful, if not laboured, pictures. To begin with, the artist built up broad masses of shadow: very black, dark and dense. He then painted his light passages on top of the

black layers in opaque blocks of colour with a lot of white pigment mixed in, not just to indicate blue sky seen between branches, or leaves catching the sun against shadow, but painting all the light areas on dark so that a black outline is left by implication. The black tones exaggerate the lightness of the bright patches, giving an almost stained-glass effect. The distinct patchwork of colours catches the dappling of strong sunlight through thick foliage, the shadows on the grass and path, and the folds and patterns of the clothes. Bright impasto plaques of cobalt blue and white are physically on top of the dark drawing of the branches and trunks and yet optically recede behind it.

The sharply accentuated and differentiated patches of light and dark are evidently influenced by black-and-white photography. Indeed the *Garden* is said to have been engendered from photographs shown by Bazille to Monet from the former's family album. Bazille's own painting of 1867, *The Family Reunion (Réunion de famille)*, clearly springs from such a group photograph, but as an essay in out-of-doors portraiture, this painting was clearly inspired by Monet's *Garden*. However, whereas Bazille's picture is frozen, static, Monet's women are enjoying a sedate, grown-up romp.

Monet returned to Paris to finish his large canvas in Bazille's studio. His parents had by then cut off his allowance. The Salon refused to take his picture, and Bazille bought it for 2,500 francs, which he arranged to pay to Monet in monthly instalments of 50 francs as a kind of allowance.

In addition to money worries, Monet had other problems: Camille was pregnant. Monet revealed her existence and her state of health to his family in the hope that their sympathy would be aroused, and Bazille tried to help by writing a supportive letter to Monet's father. However, in return for their assistance, the family imposed conditions to which Monet had no option but to agree: he was to go to live with his aunt at Sainte-Adresse, adjoining Le Havre; Camille was to be left behind in Paris in the care of his friends. He wrote humiliating, begging letters to Bazille and others, asking for money, and was not even able to return to Paris for the birth of his son Jean, to whom Bazille was godfather. In addition, Monet had eye trouble and could not paint out of doors, but he was stubborn, and would do nothing else to earn a living.

When he had left Ville d'Avray, he had abandoned nearly 200 pictures. His friends retrieved some of them for him, but he scraped down these canvases in Normandy in order to have something

Claude Monet 1868

to paint on. No one knows how much work was lost at this time, and its nature can only be guessed at. Pride and despair led him to be aggressive and truculent to his friends. In 1868, he wrote a letter to Bazille saying that he was considering suicide.

Then came some relief. In the spring of 1868, Boudin managed to obtain an invitation for Monet to send work to an International Maritime Exhibition at Le Havre. Monet received favourable notices and won a silver medal. His name was becoming known. A Le Havre shipowner, Monsieur Gaudibert, commissioned Monet to paint a portrait of his wife, and the picture was begun in September. Until that date, however, Monet and his little family continued to suffer distress: Monet was thrown out of an hotel at Fécamp, north of Le Havre, because he could not pay his bill; his canvases at Le Havre were impounded and sold by creditors; the baby was ill; Monet had to badger Bazille for his 50-franc payments.

Monet's first concern in the portrait of Madame Gaudibert was to please his client. He literally could not afford to be provocative. Two years earlier, Monet's life-size portrait of Camille, *Woman in a Green Dress (Femme au manteau vert)* had been accepted by the Salon, and Emile Zola had commended it for its dash and vigour (Monet claimed to have painted it in four days). It was now Monet's intention to show that he could paint formal portraits, and the *Green Dress* was certainly instrumental in gaining him the Gaudibert commission. This latter work is well within the conventions of portrait painting save for Madame Gaudibert's head – her face is half hidden in lost profile, her features barely visible. This may be the result of difficulties that Monet had with the portrait, or it may have been a personal whim of his, an attempt to imply movement or an air of informality. (What his clients thought of this has gone unrecorded.) He paid much more attention to the stiff, grey silk dress and oriental shawl.

It is a harmonious, sweet study in quiet grey tones enlivened by the dusky reds of the shawl, the orange braid on the curtain forming the background and the pale orange-pink roses in a vase on the black lacquered table. A contemporary critic might have said that Monet was gradually overcoming his clumsiness and coming to terms with paint, that he was within striking distance of the slick finish with a hint of bravura required of the conventional portrait painter of the time.

If our idea of Impressionism encompasses a light touch, separate brush strokes divided between colours, a brilliant effusion of light, atmospheric rendering and suggestion rather than statement, then we look in vain for traces of Impressionism in Monet's work at this time, not only in a deliberately subdued portrait such as this, but in the surviving landscapes painted for his own personal reasons. One such survives from the studies for the *Déjeuner*, the *Bas Bréau Road (Le chemin de Bas Bréau)* of 1865. Painted on the spot, it has sparkle, and the light – a pervasive grey-yellow filtering through the trees painted *contre jour* – is really the subject of the simple composition rather than the 'view', which is an empty stage waiting for action. We might expect to find much more freedom and experiment in such personal pictures, but they are carried out with the same precision of carefully mixed, solid blocks of colour as in the Gaudibert portrait. Indeed, the colour in these is subordinated to the tone, and really comprises a series of grey tints,

Opposite: *Portrait of Mme. Gaudibert*
1868 Oil on canvas
216 x 138 cm (85 x $54\frac{3}{8}$ in)
Musée d'Orsay, Paris
Monet obviously wanted to give the portrait a rather casual air by having his sitter turn away from the painter.

Above: *Camille: Woman in a Green Dress*
1866 Oil on canvas
231 x 151 cm (91 x $59\frac{2}{5}$ in)
Künsthalle, Bremmen
Here the half-turned head of Camille implies she is turning towards, not away from us.

mixtures of predominantly black and white in which the colour is heavily diluted. The work of Boudin looks far more Impressionistic than this.

We expect a painting to be, so to speak, the last word about itself. Ultimately, all interpretation exhausted, we return to the picture to see what it has to say for itself. We must be on guard against too much comment, suspicious of wordiness, of seeing or being taught to see what is not there. Impressionism itself has taught that. Yet the pictures themselves can deceive.

It might well be expected, for example, that a picture painted on the spot would be sketchy, rough and ready, painted in a great hurry against the clock, changes in time of day, light and weather, struggling against factors not under the artist's control, the artist having to work in haste to capture that specific point in time, place and space. The studio picture, on the other hand, should be well finished, reflecting a calm atmosphere in which the painter can take his time, carefully considering each deliberate step, and brought to the finish as required by the artist, not dictated by failing light or falling leaves. In fact, it is often the converse that is true. Take the classic case of John Constable. His paintings on the spot are

Above: *Bas Bréau Road*
1865 Oil on canvas
42 x 59 cm (16½ x 23¼ in)
Musée d'Orsay, Paris
This landscape dates from the period that Monet spent at Chailly painting his picnic.

stolid, solid and grey, while the set-piece pictures worked up from these studies in the secure privacy of his painting room were carried out with apparent abandon, as if dashed off hurriedly to capture the passing moment. This has caused much confusion in dating his Weymouth Bay pictures, for example.

Top: John Constable.
Weymouth Bay
*c.*1816 Oil on canvas
53.3 x 74.9 cm (21 x 29½ in)
National Gallery, London
This has all the hallmarks of a studio picture, but may well be the result of matching tones as seen on the spot.

Above: John Constable.
Weymouth Bay
*c.*1816 Oil on millboard
20.3 x 24.7 cm (8 x 9¾ in)
Victoria and Albert Museum, London
Constable often painted his freer, spontaneous sketches in the studio.

Top: Diagram. *Traditionally, painters followed the same technique for landscapes as for figure painting, drawing the scene in dark transparent washes of brown paint, then varying the thickness of the finished painting.*

Above: Diagram. *Constable and Turner worked on a toned ground. This diagram shows how Constable left the background to show through in the shadows, working quickly in broad gestures of paint.*

Imagine an artist painting on the spot. He sets up his canvas and gets off to a quick start, blocking in the subject in simplified tones, the sky and clouds, distance, middle distance, foreground. Bright clouds on a blue-grey sky, or dark clouds on a light sky, distant blues, then – darkest of all – a row of trees, and light reflected from grass or earth broken by dark shadows. Then he starts to refine, adding accents and details. The first quick layer is a kind of intuitive guesswork, rough

estimates to be corrected later. The artist stops and assesses what he has done so far, comparing his painted tones with what he sees in front of him. He then takes up his brushes again, adjusting, altering, compromising. At each stage, he hopes to take a step closer to his intention, the finished picture. At the same time, the longer he looks, the more he sees. It is difficult to avoid being dictated to by the subject, and the picture will tend to become more and more detailed. Meanwhile, he is chasing the elusive changing tones, constantly lightening here, darkening there, painting wet paint into wet paint. Thinly at first, but thicker and thicker as the paint builds up and he feels the need to obliterate his previous essays. The paint will become denser, more opaque, thicker and greyer.

The Petit Bras in Spring
1872 Oil on canvas
52.6 x 71.8 cm (20¾ x 28½ in)
National Gallery, London
The Petit Bras of the Seine ran behind the Ile Marante just below the little town of Argenteuil. Monet's painting is of a misty winter's day with a hint of spring in the trees, and the town in violet silhouette on the horizon.

Perversely, it is indoors in the studio that our artist finds freedom. Here he paints not what he sees but what he knows. A combination of knowledge and memory will filter out some details and emphasize others. The view remains recognizable, but his vision of it is more personal. What is relevant to his picture will be irrelevant to another artist, who will only remember what is relevant to him. When our artist has what he wants, he stops. In the open air, the light changes, the shadows move, the land itself seems to shift while he looks at it and he runs on the spot simply to stay where he is. In the studio, all is as much under his control as his skill in painting will allow.

This is an oversimplification of a complex process. When the artist arrives at his 'formula' in the studio – for all painting is that, a stylized approximation to imply what is seen – that formula, which is more or less personal according to experience and maturity, is then carried with him in his head, his eyes and his hand and applied on the spot. Gradually, there is a closer unity between open-air studies and work finished in the studio. There must be something of this process in the development of all landscape artists. We see its progress in Turner and Constable, and in Boudin and Monet. Something like it happened in the development of Impressionism generally. In the two years before 1870, a significant change can be seen in Monet's painting. One reason for this is the fact that Monet and Renoir worked side by side at Bougival on the river Seine, just outside Paris, where there was a popular bathing station called La Grenouillère ('the frog pond'). There is no doubt that Monet learned much from Renoir, who always worked with a light, deft touch. This was the result of his early years as a china painter, when the ability to use a single brush stroke in the right place with absolute accuracy was essential. Fumbling would spoil the work, and moreover a china painter was paid by piecework at a very low rate, and could not afford to falter, and had no time for correction or alteration. Renoir put his skill to good use in

painting fans and decorative screens and blinds; still paid on a low rate of piecework, he had to be fast and accurate to earn anything like a living. Consequently, Renoir never displayed the heavy-handedness apparent in the work of Monet, Pissarro or Cézanne.

In addition, during his student days, Monet would have learned, if he had been taught anything at all, to work in simple blocks of tone in emphatic planes and limited colour – tenets found in the teaching of Carolus Durand and followed by Manet, who considered it a virtue to use as few colours on the palette as possible. Durand's teaching, described in great detail by R.M. Stevenson, cousin of Robert Louis and a painting student in Paris, emphasized a deliberate sequence of stages, each clearly defined, from the general to the particular, and founded on direct observation of the subject. Durand was the most liberal of the Establishment painters and a gifted, serious teacher who, in his own work, stopped short of where his teaching led. His influence and methods can be clearly seen in Monet's first major works.

Freedom may have equally come to Monet not only from his seeing Renoir at work but by what he painted when he was with him. Monet had always been attracted by the subject of water, but at La Grenouillère, he was not painting monumental waves breaking on a beach in the manner of Courbet, but small, even ripples, always in movement, always changing but always repeating themselves in the same place, a phenomenon that we can all see for ourselves.

In order to understand painting, it is not only necessary to look long and hard at the paintings themselves but also at the painter's subjects, trying to see them with a painter's eye. Water is no exception. For example, Antonio Canaletto found a quite mechanical formula for reproducing wavelets on the Venice lagoon – for all the world like parallels of linked hand-written double-Us

Opposite: *Bathers at La Grenouillère*
1869 Oil on canvas
73 x 92 cm (28¾ x 36¼ in)
National Gallery, London
One of a series painted at the bathing station on the river Seine west of Paris, and all distinguished by a boldness of execution with thick blobs of paint.

Top: August Renoir.
La Grenouillère
1869 Oil on canvas
65 x 93 cm (25⅗ x 36⅗ in)
Sammlung Oskar Reinhart Am Römerholz, Winterthur
Renoir, who had developed a delicate touch as a china decorator, is more fluid than Monet who is quite rough in his efforts to achieve feedom.

in thin white paint on grey-blue. At the proper viewing distance, these dissolve into light on water, and can actually be seen on still but wind-touched waters. If we look at a view long enough, the apparent random reflections of light and dark on the fluid surface repeat themselves over and over again into a static pattern like the standing waves on a system of mechanical vibrations as in a pendulum. This is what such wavelets are.

Endeavouring to capture this amorphous surface in paint on canvas, Monet resorted to the use of broken brush strokes of separate unblended tones and colours. The subjects that he now painted dictated the technique to him just as the wind-blown beaches of the Channel coast had dictated the method to Boudin. Whatever Monet may have learned from Renoir – and indeed sometimes, when looking at their work completed during this period, it is difficult to tell them apart – there was an even stronger element of self-discovery and rediscovery. The first phase of Monet's work was coming to an end.

Bazille continued to bear Monet's demands and hard words with patience, although in exasperation, he was moved to tell Monet, who was desperate to get a job like anyone else, 'Go and chop wood.' Despite this, in 1870, Renoir and Monet moved into Bazille's old studio, for which he still paid the rent, while he himself took a second studio in the Rue de la Condamine. His painting of the interior of this studio with his friends (overleaf) gives us a very good idea of how these painters lived. The figure standing on the stairs is the writer Emile Zola, who is talking to Renoir, perched on the edge of the table below him, Manet is looking at the painting on the easel while Monet looks on. The tall figure of Bazille, standing by his picture, was painted in by Manet.

That June, Monet married Camille, and after the wedding, they went to Trouville where Monet painted a series of seaside pictures. The Franco-Prussian war broke out in July, and disaster and defeat was followed by the Commune and civil war in Paris. Bazille was called up, and Renoir was conscripted into the cavalry; Manet and Degas joined the National Guard. Cézanne evaded conscription and hid in the south; Pissarro and Monet fled to London (Camille and Jean stayed behind with Boudin). Left empty, Pissarro's house at Louveciennes in the Paris suburbs was

Ships at Anchor on the Seine at Rouen
1872 Oil on canvas
37.8 x 46.6 cm (14⅞ x 18⅜ in)
National Gallery of Art, Washington D.C. Ailsa Mellon Bruce Collection
Rouen was an important inland port with interchange traffic between sea-going ships and canal and river barges. The ships are barquentines with a mixed square and fore and aft rig much used in the coastal trade. The spire of Rouen cathedral can be glimpsed on the left.

commandeered by the Prussian army who used the ground floor as an abattoir. The house not only contained all Pissarro's work of the previous 15 years, but a considerable number of Monet's paintings, which he had stored there to keep them out of the hands of his creditors. The soldiers used the canvases as oil cloth mats to keep their feet dry.

On arriving in London, Monet met up with the landscape painter Charles Daubigny (1817–78), and he introduced Monet to the dealer Paul Durand-Ruel, also a refugee. Durand-Ruel had clients in England, and Daubigny persuaded him

Frédéric Bazille. *The Studio of the Painter*
1870 Oil on canvas
92 × 128 cm (36 1/5 × 50 2/5 in)
Musée d'Orsay, Paris
Bazille's painting of his friends is a marvellous record of the way the painters lived and worked.

Charles-François Daubigny. *St. Paul's Cathedral from the Surrey side*
1873 Oil on canvas
44 × 81.3 cm (17 3/8 × 32 in)
National Gallery, London

Above: *The Beach at Trouville*
1870 Oil on canvas
37.5 × 45.7cm (14 3/4 × 18 in)
Tate Gallery, London
In June 1870 Monet married Camille Doncieux and they spent the early summer at Trouville. Monet painted a series of studies of Camille on the beach, boldly designed and broadly painted 'snap shots'.

to stock paintings by Monet. Durand-Ruel was to become Monet's primary dealer and was to lay the foundation for Monet's later prosperity. From him, Monet learned that Pissarro was staying with his half-sister who had married an Englishman and lived in the London suburb of Dulwich near the Crystal Palace on Sydenham Hill. Julie Vellay, who had been Pissarro's mother's housemaid, was with him, pregnant with their third child. Pissarro married her during this English sojourn.

London seemed a strange place to the artists. No one had heard of them, or indeed of any other French painters. There were no artists' cafés or anywhere else where artists, writers and students gathered and where they could make themselves known. All social life took place in private houses from which strangers were excluded. The Royal Academy rejected their work, even though by now

they were being accepted quite regularly, if grudgingly, by the Salon.

Yet despite the discouraging atmosphere, both Pissarro and Monet were to become regular visitors to London. Pissarro's family settled there and his sons went to school in the capital; he painted the Crystal Palace, Dulwich College and the railway at Lordship Lane station. Monet returned again and again to stay at the Savoy and paint Hyde Park and the Thames at Charing Cross and Westminster. In his first Westminster picture, the riverside pier and the Houses of Parliament are silhouetted in a typical yellow-ochre light of coal smoke and sulphur fumes.

The two artists saw the work of Constable and Turner and were impressed. Whether they were influenced, as is sometimes claimed, is another matter. Their work was so far removed technically from that of the English painters that, much as they might admire them, there was little they could learn from and use.

The war ended, the Commune fell, and the painters gradually came back from their various places of refuge or from the army – all except Bazille, who had been killed in action. Paris had been shattered by bombardments, decimated by executions and starvation, and the nation was bankrupt, burdened by war reparations. The artists had begun to sell regularly, if not well, but enough to be encouraged through dealers such as Durand-Ruel, and they hoped to get back to where they had left off. They were to be disappointed. The Parisians, upon whose patronage they had largely depended, now had other things to think about. It was thus that the idea of selling directly to the public through an

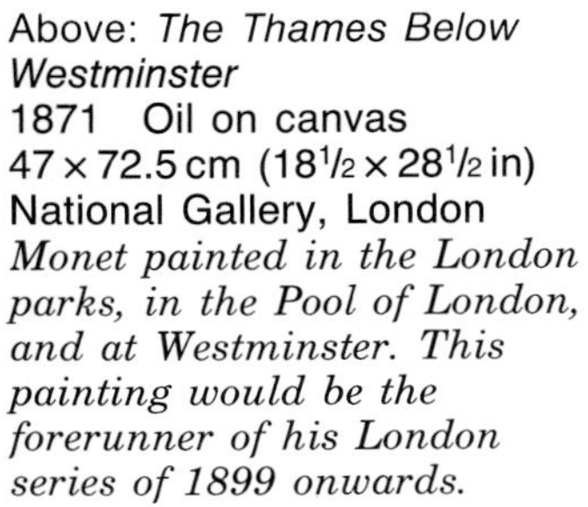

Above: *The Thames Below Westminster*
1871 Oil on canvas
47 x 72.5 cm (18½ x 28½ in)
National Gallery, London
Monet painted in the London parks, in the Pool of London, and at Westminster. This painting would be the forerunner of his London series of 1899 onwards.

Top right: Camille Pissarro. *Lordship Lane Station*
1871 Oil on canvas
45 x 74 cm (17¾ x 29⅛ in)
Courtauld Institute Galleries, London
This suburban railway station, formerly thought to be Penge, was close to Upper Norwood and the Crystal Palace where Pissarro lodged.

Above: John Constable. *Study for Cirrus Clouds*
Undated. Oil on paper
11.4 x 17.8 cm (4½ x 7 in)
Victoria and Albert Museum, London
Monet and Pissarro saw paintings by Turner and Constable during their visit to London, and were impressed, but probably not influenced by them. Constable worked rapidly, making his cloud studies on the spot, but he relied on the classical technique, making full use of light brushwork upon a toned ground.

exhibition of their own was revived. Bazille had proposed the idea as early as 1867, but it had come to nothing for lack of support. Two years later, he had made a second attempt but this had been frustrated by the outbreak of the war in which he died.

In May 1873, Paul Alexis, a journalist and friend of Zola, reported in the newspaper *L'Avenir national* that he had received a letter from Monet saying that a group of painters had formed an exhibiting society and hoped for journalistic support. A year was to pass before they got themselves organized, but on 15 April 1874 they opened their exhibition in Nadar's studio,

deliberately coinciding with the date of the annual Salon.

With hindsight, it can be said that they mistimed their venture. Nearly ten years had elapsed since the famous Salon des Refusés which their Société Anonyme wished to re-create, and the sympathy that the Salon des Refusés had aroused, together with the royal patronage it had received, had gone, discredited. The deposed emperor (who died in January 1873) was held personally responsible for the disasters of 1870 and the aftermath. The public was all for reconstruction and a return to stability and the status quo, not for experiment and adventures. The Société Anonyme was not only bypassing the Salon and its jury but the dealers as well, and the latter were not very pleased. Durand-Ruel, for example, had invested over 70,000 francs in the work of Monet, Pissarro and others, and was patiently trying to create a market. The last thing he wanted was adverse publicity that would frighten people off.

Manet, the Impressionists' senior painter, refused to have anything to do with the scheme. He was at last beginning to be a success in Salon circles, and defended his refusal by saying that the battle should be fought in the Salon, not outside it; the decision to go it alone could only make matters worse. Degas for his part insisted that work by established but conventional painters should be included.

Monet exhibited two major paintings and some pastel sketches. His *Port of Le Havre in Mist (Impression: A Sunrise) – Le Port du Havre par la brume (Impression: Soleil levant)* unwittingly gave the group and its work the nickname which has stuck ever since, a word with the same imprecise meaning as the fleeting glimpse it was meant to imply. It was the most Turneresque of Monet's paintings and did much to encourage

speculation about the influence on him of Turner's paintings, which he had seen during his London visit of 1870. There are some similarities. Like Monet, Turner had been fond of making the sun the centre of his compositions. Monet was to do the same again in his *Sunset on the Seine in Winter (Soleil couchant sur la Seine: éffet d'hiver)*, dated 1880 and exhibited in 1882. A critic's comparison

of Monet's sun to slice of tomato stuck on to the sky is reminiscent of similar criticisms made at Turner's expense. But the resemblance is entirely a superficial one.

Turner employed colour theory, as did Monet, but Turner was pre-Chevreul, and took his model from Goethe. Goethe was at pains to emphasize the oneness, the unity of nature, and the

Opposite top: Paul Cézanne.
Paul Alexis Reading a Manuscript to Emile Zola
*c.*1869 – 70 Oil on canvas
131 × 161 cm (51 3/5 × 63 2/5 in)
Museu de Arte, São Paolo
Emile Zola and his colleague and disciple Paul Alexis were champions of the Impressionists' cause.

Above: *Sunset at Lavacourt*
1880 Oil on canvas
100 × 152 cm (39 3/8 × 59 7/8 in)
Musée du Petit Palais, Paris
Monet declared, 'This canvas is much too much to my personal taste to send to the Salon'. It is remarkable in its complementary similarity to his Impression.

phenomenon of light was to him the model of economy in action. According to the German poet, all light is one, and colour varies according to the density and transparency of the surfaces it encounters. This absolutely fits the classical painters' technique which Turner still used. It must also be borne in mind that Turner, almost from the outset of his career while still in his teens, was a highly trained and skilled watercolour painter. He did not use watercolour simply as an adjunct to his oil painting – for sketching on the spot, getting a quick reference for a finished studio piece – but used it as a major technique in itself. This strongly influenced his work in oils, which was fluid and wash-like in his atmospheric paintings.

Monet followed the colour theory of Chevreul, based on the observation of colour harmonies and contrasts in dyes and pigments, not in nature. The blue sky in *A Sunrise* is not the implied, atmospheric blue of a wash upon a warm ground but a dense blue pigment, providing maximum contrast to the orange-red disc of the sun. The suggested details of cranes, ships' funnels and rigging, the skeins of steam and smoke are painted in thinner, darker streaks using a long-haired sable brush known to marine artists as a 'rigger'. Variations in the sky and the water are also painted in thin brush strokes and dabs, not watery washes. The ripples on the harbour basin, reflecting the rising sun and counter-shaded against it, are dashes of solid paint that seem to float across the surface, emphasizing depth and perspective.

The sketchy nature of the painting worried the critics intensely. If a picture is left unfinished, they argued, there must be a reason. This could be that the painter has bitten off more than he could chew and had given up. He could have reached a technical impasse or had a mental block. Or it could be incompetence: the painter, having gained some sort of effect, was unable to finish the painting and was afraid of spoiling it or showing himself up by his lack of ability. This could lead quite naturally to a defiant gesture, to the artist bluffing his way by claiming that his work as it stood was exactly what he had always intended. If one cannot see detailed drawing in a painting, said the critics, then it is obvious that the artist cannot draw. Otherwise he would be only too ready to demonstrate his skill.

Critics and public were used to sketches by artists. They appreciated them and collected them. But they expected them to be studies for a finished work to which they could be related and which would give them legitimacy. They were not prepared for a free study to be a work of art in its own right. Turner was acceptable at the Royal

J.M.W. Turner. *Sun Rising Through Vapour*
1807 Oil on canvas
69 × 102 cm (27 1/8 × 40 1/8 in)
Barber Institute of Fine Arts, University of Birmingham
'The sun is god.' Legend has it that these were Turner's last words. But rather than being the forerunner of Impressionism, Turner was the last and greatest of the pre-19th century painters who lived on into the industrial age. He pushed the classical technique to the limit where it dissolved. When Monet was asked about Turner, he commented that he disliked Turner's exuberant romanticism.

Above: *Bridge at Argenteuil on a Grey Day*
1876 Oil on canvas
61 × 80.3 cm (24 × 31³/₅ in)
National Gallery of Art, Washington D.C. Ailsa Mellon Bruce Collection
Monet shows the floating pier with its office-cum-shed, the landing stage and sailing boat, and to the right, his little floating studio, the hut on a boat. Beyond is the arched round bridge, repaired after the war, which Monet usually painted in steep perspective.

Right: Diagram. *This mock Turner shows how the painter worked in the pre-19th century way. His underpainting became lighter and redder, and his final layers of paint were applied in increasingly thinner washes, but his misty impressions use the same techniques of optical effects as the Renaissance painters.*

Diagram. *This cloud sketch demonstrates the optical mixing of colour in thin films, as in the red underpaintings that Constable and Turner worked in.*

Diagram. *By contrast an Impressionist painting would be in solid blocks of colour all over, increasing in thickness with each addition of tone and colour as the painter matches paint with light and shade.*

Academy in London because he could successfully demonstrate that he could draw and finish too, but this did not make his later work any more popular or understandable. 'Tinted steam, and very like,' said the critics.

Conventionally, a painter worked on his picture in distinct stages from start to finish: first an outline drawing, then blocking in with monochrome shading, then various layers of colours, tints and glazes, with more detail added each time towards the finished, varnished work. The work could be said to progress, in the exact sense of the word – to grow, advancing from the general to the particular. If the picture was abandoned at any intermediate stage for one reason or another, it was, and looked, unfinished.

However, Monet and his fellow painters no longer worked quite like that. Painting on the spot, or in the studio as if they were working on the spot, they set down their observations – it is tempting to say 'impressions' – as they went along, working all over the canvas at once, from the start trying to match paint with the subject, re-touching, refining and modifying. Thus, and this is a major difference, each stage is a complete statement in its own right. When the painter had found what he wanted, he simply stopped. The work was finished. If he were working on a series of pictures on the same subject – Monet is an example *par excellence* of this – he may in one picture arrive at his target quickly, but in the next, it may elude him and he would have to re-work layer after layer. This has caused, and still causes, confusion about what is a finished work and what is not.

For instance, Paul Cézanne (1839–1906) frequently left large areas of unpainted white canvas. Do we conclude from this that these paintings were abandoned as unfinishable, or that he had lost interest, or that they were, for him, simply finished? They now take their place in the great collections, so that we can assume that, to the present-day gallery-goer, they are acceptable statements by a great master in their own right. In Cézanne's own time, they gave rise to absurd legends about his abandoning hopeless canvases in hedgerows and ditches, where people waited to snap them up. As is so often the case, the question of finished or unfinished became a moral one, clouding the issue of appreciating each picture on its own merits.

The second of Monet's major works that appeared in the exhibition of 1874 was his *Boulevard des Capucines* (1873). This view of the street from Nadar's upstairs window is a more substantial work, and to a certain extent, its technique is different from that of the *Sunrise*. For one thing, the background is quite densely painted. It seems that Monet rendered the perspective view of the street, the buildings and the row of trees in some finished detail and then literally half-obliterated this in a mist of paint in his search for atmosphere. Having arrived at the required dissolution of façades and branches into blue mist, he then painted in the figures and other foreground details in transparent touches of dark blue-black paint. Ernest Chesnau of the *Paris Journal* was enthusiastic: 'The extraordinary animation of the public street, the crowded pavements, the carriages, the trees shimmering in dust and light, never has movement's illusive quality been captured in all its fluidity as in this extraordinarily marvellous sketch. At a distance one hails a masterpiece . . . but come closer, and it all vanishes.

Boulevard des Capucines
1873 Oil on canvas
61 x 80.3 cm (24 x 31 3/5 in)
Pushkin Museum of Fine Art, Moscow
The critic, Louis Leroy complained of the innumerable black tongue lickings in the lower part of the picture, but a colleague, Ernest Chesnau wrote, 'Never has movement's illusive quality been captured in all its fluidity'.

There remains only an indecipherable chaos of palette scrapings.'

Here is an intelligent and supportive critic who puts the public dilemma in a nutshell: marvellous though it is, the picture is an illusion that only too easily dissolves into a mess, a sketch which must be transformed into a finished work. But what a bugle call for those who listen carefully! A forerunner, then, a hint. But more than a hint.

Louis Leroy, writing for the satirical paper *Charivari*, asked, 'Be so good as to tell me what those innumerable black tongue-lickings are in the lower part of the picture . . . I'll get a stroke from it, I'm sure.' He advised pregnant women and invalids to stay away.

In the eyes of the public, the artists were not only trying to sell unfinished work, but their prices were not cheap: encouraged by his little success of previous years, Monet asked 1,000 francs for his *Sunrise.* The exhibition did so badly that the Société Anonyme was forced to go into liquidation. Its members held an auction at the Hôtel Drouot to raise money to pay the debt, but the sensationalism of the press notices made collectors nervous and paintings sold for half the price that similar works had previously fetched.

In spite of such setbacks, the original group from the defunct Société returned to the attack, holding another exhibition in 1876. It seemed that they could sell their work in no other way. Durand-Ruel had been badly hit by a bank failure and was bankrupt, but he tried to do what he could for his stable of painters, in kind if not in cash, by lending them his gallery premises in the Rue le Pelletier. Unlike the previous exhibition, which had been chosen by a committee that had tried to leaven the unconventional with the conventional, the painters were hung in block groupings of their own work. Monet showed 18 pictures: 17 landscapes and a fancy-dress portrait of Camille, *La Japonaise.* This exhibition caused less scandal. Among those who wrote serious reviews of it were Emile Zola and the poet Stéphane Mallarmé, while less expected were the reviews by the novelist Henry James and the dramatist August Strindberg. Zola described Monet as 'incontestably the head of the group'. He singled out the *Japonaise* for particular attention, and it was generally much admired.

It seems beyond doubt that, in this work, the desperate Monet was making another bid for fashionable bourgeois clients. It is a strange, forced, uncomfortable picture with an almost hysterical air of strained gaiety. In Paris, there was a vogue for things Japanese: fans, ceramics,

Opposite top: *La Japonaise. Mme. Monet in Japanese Costume*
1875 Oil on canvas
231.6 x 142.3 cm (91 1/5 x 56 in)
Museum of Fine Arts, Boston, Massachusetts
Monet was always in a desperate financial situation, not helped by habitually living beyond his means. Something of this desperation comes across in this picture, with its highly artificial composition and its air of forced gaiety. Monet had always been successful with his 'fancy dress' portraits, and was trying everything in this picture, including the fashion for things Japanese.

Opposite bottom: Edouard Manet. *Portrait of Emile Zola*
1868 Oil on canvas
146.5 x 114 cm (57 5/8 x 44 7/8 in)
Musée d'Orsay, Paris
Manet's portrait of Zola was an act of gratitude, repaying the writer for his support in the press. The novelist is in his study, at his desk. Behind him is a Japanese screen; on the wall is an Utamaro print of an actor, together with Velasquez's Topers *and an engraving of* Olympia.

Right: *Woman with a Parasol. Mme. Monet and her Son*
1875 Oil on canvas
100 x 81 cm (39 3/8 x 31 7/8 in)
National Gallery of Art, Washington D.C.
Mr. and Mrs. Paul Mellon Collection
In this painting, also known as The Promenade, *Camille and Jean are outlined against a summer sky on a meadow bank of grasses and wild flowers. The picture is as delicate, personal, and tasteful as the* Japonaise *is false.*

woodcut prints, hybrid chrysanthemums. As an attempt to exploit this craze, Monet's painting is crude and vulgar by comparison with Manet's tribute to Japan in his portrait of Zola, or Van Gogh's transcriptions of Japanese prints. The arrangement of fans seems desperately inconsequential, and the painting, finished in high detail in the padded, embroidered, grotesque figure on the kimono, is equivocal in its relationship to the living figure of the model – a kind of beauty and the beast. Camille's head, painted with a lighter, freer touch, is aesthetically detached from the rest of the painting – all the more poignant for the fact that it was Camille who bore the brunt of hardship resulting from Monet's intransigence.

There can be no greater contrast than between this highly artificial picture, the star of the show, and *The Promenade, Woman with a Parasol (La Promenade, Femme à l'ombrelle)* (1875), featuring Camille Monet and her son Jean. Freely painted and yet finished to perfection, the painting is full of light and air, as natural as nature itself. The spectator can almost feel the light breeze that flutters the drapery of a summer dress, and hear the sibilant rustle of the grasses. Those looking for tradition in the visual arts might favourably compare Monet's portrayal of the draped figure with classical sculpture or a Tanagra terracotta

figurine. She is painted against the light, *contre jour*, in beautifully observed tone edged by a luminous halo. The composition is deceptively casual, a snapshot view carefully calculated to achieve movement and spontaneity. The green-lined parasol is cut by the edge of the canvas. Steep perspective from Camille's head to that of the child is reinforced by the sharply diminishing clouds, which we can so easily imagine moving behind the figure in the windy sky. But technically the most interesting passage is the foreground where Camille's shadow is cast across the grass bank straight towards the viewer.

In Monet's *Women in the Garden*, the shadows falling across grass are carefully and solidly painted in blocks of uniform tone, rigidly designed and fitted like a jigsaw puzzle. Here the brush work is broken and streaky, echoing and reproducing the linear tangle of the blades of grass. The colour is broken, too. There are increasingly fine touches of pure colour, not merely a variety of brilliant greens, but green-yellows, bright pure yellow, light-blue, red. In the sunlit passages, green-yellow and yellow strokes predominate in the topmost layers; in the shadows, blue-green, green and red-brown. But the sunlit area also

Above: *Autumn Effect. Argenteuil*
1873 Oil on canvas
56 x 75 cm (22 x 29½ in)
Courtauld Institute Galleries, London
This painting glitters with touches of thick impasto paint. Monet used the handle of his brush to scratch the textures of the lighter branches in the right-hand clump of trees

Left: *Argenteuil*
1872 Oil on canvas
50.4 x 65.2 cm (19⅞ x 25⅝ in)
National Gallery of Art, Washington D.C. Ailsa Mellon Bruce Collection
In this early view of the promenade at Argenteuil Monet kept his horizon low, at the spectator's eye level, so that one is led into the picture along the towpath.

contains the blue range of colours, and the shadow the yellows. The colours are not blended into overall blocks or masses to match light and shade. Our eyes mix the strands at the normal viewing distance while being aware of their separation. As in nature, the light contains dark and the shade light. This division of tone and colour, using small touches of brilliant colour to imply soft, harmonious, 'natural' colours was to become the focal point of Monet's study of light.

Just how much this was the result of Monet learning from Chevreul's work on colour is difficult to say. It is safe to assume that he was introduced to Chevreul's colour theory by Pissarro, for whom Chevreul's work was a bible, and with whom the division of tone and colour was to become an obsession.

The *Woman with a Parasol* is one of a series of such subjects, rather elegant scenes of sun-shaded ladies in their best dresses walking with children in fields of wild flowers with fine-weather cumulus clouds racing overhead. They were painted at Argenteuil, a village on the Seine 16 km (10 miles) from Paris by train, a popular spot with Parisians for Sunday walks, picnics and boating in spite of the river being smelly and polluted with sewage and rubbish. De Maupassant described the Seine as 'that lovely, calm, varied, striking river, full of mirages and filth'.

When Monet left war-battered Paris in 1871 to settle for the next seven years at Argenteuil, the little village was already on its way to becoming an industrial suburb. A foundry, a chemical works, cement works and a tannery were adding to the pollution. The road and rail bridges, often featured in Monet's paintings, had been blown up by the Prussians and were being rebuilt. Monet found a house with a garden, where he lived in some style, with two housemaids and a gardener, but was always on the verge of debt. Here he could indulge his passion for horticulture, and concentrated on painting the little vineyards still remaining and the poppy fields. He also had a little boat converted into a floating studio on the river.

Argenteuil was popular with fellow painters, too. It was almost a symbol, a survival of a fast-

Above left: Edouard Manet. *Monet Painting in his Studio Boat*
1874 Oil on canvas
82.5 × 100.4 cm ($32^1/_2$ × $39^1/_2$ in)

Left: August Renoir. *Monet Painting in his Garden at Argenteuil*
1873 Oil on canvas
46.7 × 59.7 cm ($18^3/_8$ × $23^1/_2$ in)
Wadsworth Athenaeum, Hartford, Connecticut. Anne Parrish Titzell Bequest

Above right: *Train in Snow*
1875 Oil on canvas
59 × 78 cm ($23^1/_4$ × $30^3/_4$ in)
Musée Marmottan, Paris

vanishing rural idyll, a product of the townsman's imagination. Manet came and painted Monet working in his boat. Renoir painted Monet at an easel in his garden. Renoir and Monet again worked side by side, painting sailing boats waiting for hire by the bridge, and the Argenteuil regatta, which had progressed from a rough affair to a smart event. By de Maupassant's own account, the railway brought not the fashionable, quiet Parisians who strolled in the Bois de Boulogne or Tuileries but rowdy hooligans, a form of human pollution to match the city's waste flowing downstream. For Monet, however, Argenteuil was a little paradise that nothing could disturb.

It is sometimes difficult to tell apart Monet's and Renoir's work from this period. Monet's touch became freer. Still working in dark tones occasionally, obviously mixing paint into paint on the spot, he was also beginning not just to paint light but trying to paint with light, to render the *enveloppe*, that all-embracing, mysterious bubble of atmosphere that pervaded the subject. And one subject that figured strongly was the railway.

He had already painted a number of pictures with a railway subject: a local train during his days at Bougival, and a suburban train in the snow in 1875, a close-toned painting in grey and yellow-ochre mixtures, with the little locomotive in silhouette at Argenteuil, its orange-yellow oil lamps shining in the half-light. The railway bridge at Argenteuil, an inelegant girder bridge on heavy cylindrical piers, very close in appearance to Charing Cross Bridge on the Thames, and which carried the railway from Paris to Le Havre, featured conspicuously in his paintings of the river. He could easily have ignored this intruder into the landscape as he did the factories nearby. To include it was a deliberate act. We may assume, then, that railways held a certain attraction for Monet. Certainly, later at Giverny, he was not put off by the fact that the railway ran not by but *through* his garden, dividing his famous lily pond and semi-wild garden from his formal walks and pergolas.

The city terminus of the Western Railway (Chemins de fer de l'Ouest) was the Gare St. Lazare, and Monet commuted to Paris to paint a remarkable series of pictures in and around the station. Both the railway and the Gare St. Lazare had a special significance for Monet. His life was spent at Le Havre and Paris, the two ends of the line, and along it at Argenteuil and Giverny. Renoir, talking to his sons in old age, told the story of Monet putting on his frock coat and silk hat and calling on the superintendent of the Chemins de fer de l'Ouest at his head office and introducing himself as 'the painter Claude Monet'. Thinking that this distinguished-looking visitor must be an important Academician at the very least, the official not only granted him leave to paint, but a platform was cleared, trains were halted, and locomotives were run up and down the yard exactly where Monet wanted them, the crews cramming coal on to the fires to give out as much smoke and steam as possible.

However, not even Constable could emulate Joshua and get the sun to stand still while he painted his sunsets over Hampstead Heath, and Monet might have just as well commanded the deity to hold the light for another few minutes while he caught the effect as bring a busy railway to a halt. Not even the president of the l'Institut Français could do that. And not even the railway superintendent himself could solidify clouds of steam and smoke into static pillars for Monet's convenience.

The station throat and yard were overlooked by the company's general offices, on top of which was railwaymen's accommodation, where train crews who lived in Le Havre could spend the night before returning. There was a balcony or gallery overlooking the station, and Monet made studies from here. It is also the location of the opening scene of Emile Zola's *La Bête humaine* (1889–90), a melodramatic story of passion and jealousy between an engine driver, his wife and his fireman.

Railway Bridge at Argenteuil
1873 Oil on canvas
55 x 72 cm (21 5/8 x 28 3/8 in)
Musée d'Orsay, Paris
Standing foursquare on its solid piers, the bridge has a startling resemblance to Charing Cross bridge on the Thames, theme of one of Monet's late series.

Right: Honoré Daumier. *Les chemins de fer*
Lithograph from series
Painter and sculptor of genius, yet devoting his life to drawing for the papers, Daumier's pungent caricatures return to the railway theme time after time.

Below right: Edouard Manet. *La Gare St. Lazare*
1873 Oil on canvas
93.3 x 114.5 cm (36¾ x 45 in)
National Gallery of Art, Washington D.C. Gift of Horace Havemeyer, in memory of Louisine W. Havemeyer
Manet's Gare St. Lazare *is so much not part of the picture that one has to look twice to see the railway lines in the cutting behind the lady, her daughter, and pet dog. Once more the figures are obviously posed in Manet's studio against a background. Just to the right, between the railings, can be seen a glimpse of the Pont de l'Europe (or Pont de Rome).*

The link between Zola's novel and Monet's paintings are far more to the point than Renoir's amusing anecdote. Railway imagery was everywhere – even coffee urns and clocks were made in the form of locomotives. Honoré Daumier never tired of railway themes for his satirical lithographs. J.K. Huysmans, art critic and champion of the Impressionists, even complained that Monet's railway paintings were not realistic enough. In Huysmans' novel *A Rebours (Against Nature)*, a popular treatment of 'decadence' which Oscar Wilde envied, there is even a remarkable chapter dedicated to the technicalities of railway locomotive design.

Manet had already painted a picture called the *Gare St. Lazare*, but it is a stiffly composed studio piece of a woman and child against railings with a perfunctory back-drop of the station approach. The awkward disposition of the figures seems to imply that they are posed and painted at different times.

Monet's sequence of paintings of the Gare St. Lazare affords us an insight into his technique at this time. The paintings, which were made largely on the spot, are very badly painted with a restricted range of colour – from blue to red-brown – and what little colour there is is used to underline or reinforce warm and cold tones, light and shade. The silhouetted locomotives, the architecture of the station roofs and arches, the lamp-posts and columns and the figures are painted in direct, unbroken brush strokes. The

breadth and scale of each brush stroke is directly related to the size of the object being painted; or, to put it negatively, the passages of paint are not built up of tiny dabs of paint of uniform size regardless of what is being painted. As one might expect, the paint varies in thickness, being at its most dense in the thickly impastoed rendering of clouds of steam that obliterate the details of the structures, which are half-glimpsed through the vapour. The tonal divisions are simple and clear light-and-dark patterns, and they give the onlooker a taste of reality. The *Arrival of the Train from Normandy (Arrivée du train de Normandie)* is just such a picture.

La Gare St. Lazare. The Normandy Train
1877 Oil on canvas
59.6 × 80.2 cm (23½ × 31½ in)
Art Institute of Chicago. Mr. and Mrs. A Ryerson Collection
This canvas was painted on the spot, as its rapidly and simply blocked-in tones show. When Monet came to brush in the dark underside of the station roof, he left the area for smoke and steam white, to achieve greater transparency as he put the light, thin paint straight on to the primed canvas.

Le Pont de Rome or Pont de l'Europe, Gare St. Lazare
1877 Oil on canvas
64 × 80 cm (25⅕ × 31½ in)
Musée Marmottan, Paris
This painting of the railway yard at the entrance – or exit – to the station ran under the road bridge known variously as the Pont de l'Europe or Pont de Rome. The canvas was started on the spot, but finished in the studio with a considerable amount of overpainting to obtain the right effect of buildings, bridge and tracks seen through steam. The locomotive is an accurate representation of that driven by Zola's Lantier in La bête humaine.

Other paintings were taken a stage further, presumably in Monet's studio. The *Pont de l'Europe* (or *Pont de Rome*), now at the Musée Marmottan, is in this category. Parts of the original sketch underlying the finished picture of this pedestrian bridge over the tracks of the Gare St. Lazare can still be seen, but the picture has been refined and repainted with great care, away from the subject. Colour and tone are broken everywhere, and small strokes of paint are touched in

La Gare St. Lazare
1877 Oil on canvas
54.3 x 73.6 cm (21 3/8 x 29 in)
National Gallery, London
These selected paintings from the nine or so that Monet painted in and around the station give an immediate insight into Monet's technique, from the rapidly brushed in, very black paintings made on site and left as they are, to the reworked studio-finished canvases.

with great delicacy. Smoke and steam are no longer scrawled twists of thick impasto imitating rolling clouds, but are scumbled on to the surface of the picture in thin, translucent drifts of mist. The sky is painted in a broken mixture of colours varying from pale orange to pale blue – complementary colours that enhance each other by contrast – to give a subtle golden glow of light. The buildings, blurred by atmospheric distance, are not perfunctorily dashed in but painted in small touches with great precision. Having grasped the subject to his satisfaction quite early on in the work, the artist was subsequently at great pains to adjust each single passage of the picture to every other. Thus the picture itself, not the subject, became the dominant factor.

The masterpiece of the series, the *Gare St. Lazare*, now hanging in the Musée d'Orsay (appropriately enough, a converted railway station), almost defies description. It certainly defies reproduction, for however well the colour print is made, the work itself is always an astonishing revelation. To begin with, it seems to epitomize all that we expect of Impressionism. There is light, air, colour, movement; the picture lives and breathes. Detail is subordinated to the overall impression, the total experience caught in a moment, an instant of time fractional enough to freeze clouds of smoke and steam, to catch the moving shadow traced across a sun's ray. Yet this painting, although based on experiential reality, is entirely synthetic in construction. All trace of a sketch done on the spot – if there ever was one – has been entirely obliterated. The painting is built (there is no other word for it) from tiny blocks, spots and touches of paint. It is literally encrusted with paint, glowing like a fabulous, jewelled plaque of gold: garnets, turquoises and sapphires, with bright emerald green here and there; crimson, orange and gold; pale blue and deep ultramarine, vivid greens. All linear drawing has been painted out, and yet the finest lines are there, painted in great accuracy by touch after tiny touch. This highly artificial work could only have been carried out in the seclusion of the studio, demanding skill and knowledge with time, patience and the utmost concentration. It is a most paradoxical picture, painted with great care, almost laboriously, and yet achieving its aim: to render the impression of a moment. The form dissolves in light, and yet under scrutiny every detail is there in sharp distinction. How was this paradox achieved, this contradiction resolved?

There is a sense in which all painting is from memory. Even when the artist is working with his subject before his eyes, whether on site – in Cézanne's words, *sur le motif* – or with a still life or portrait sitter before him in his studio, at the moment when he looks away from the subject to his canvas and is faced with translating what he has seen into an equivalent in paint, he is concentrating, remembering and hazarding a touch. When working out of doors, this is even more acute, for the light is always changing, clouds move, and no two days are ever alike. The painter can chase his elusive shadows for ever, or say,

'Enough, here I stand.' He trains his memory as he trains his eye. It would be better, perhaps, to say not that he works from memory but from knowledge, for what we remember is what we know. There can be no greater authenticity than painting from knowledge, and the unique gift of painting is that, however great the artist's genius, however far his attainment seems beyond us, there is still that immediacy of recognition of common experience that binds us to him. Yes, we say, gazing at the work of which we could never have dreamed for ourselves in a lifetime, it is just like that. It was Monet's experience and knowledge that sorted out irrelevancies and subordinated detail, and concentrated on his aim and intention.

The tumbling clouds of smoke and steam that were dissolving in front of his eyes were held static in his mind's eye, which remembered distinctions between wisps of steam from idle locomotives to the blast of exhaust from an engine on the move. A beautiful example of Monet painting from

La Gare St. Lazare
1877 Oil on canvas
54.3 × 73.6 cm (21 3/8 × 29 in)
Musée d'Orsay, Paris
This is the most elaborate finished painting, worked and overworked until a jewelled crust of paint dissolves into steam and smoke, air and light.

Top detail:
Counterchange of dark figures against light, then light against dark in the shaft of sunlight. Close-up vision reveals a kaleidoscope of brilliant colour, touches of garnet-crimson, orange, light blue, sea-green, meticulously applied.

Lower detail:
Painstaking application of paint, touch by touch, is seen in the painting of the roof structure in Monet's station. Note the careful observation of tone and colour in the counterchange of the trusses, light against dark, then dark against light.

knowledge can be seen in the delicate tracery of the tie rods in the trusses of the station roof in the finished *Gare St. Lazare.* These are counter-changed, a technical term which means that the same object can simultaneously be seen partly dark against light, partly light against dark. Not only does the background change from dark to light, but the object against it changes too, in the reverse order. This is so delicately done by Monet that one has to look for it. It has been said that the real subjects of the Gare St. Lazare series are light and air, and that the station was merely a vehicle for these subtleties.

Monet's painting are not generalized or idealized pictures painted in homage to an idea, as were Turner's *Rain, Steam and Speed* and the pre-First World War Futurist railway paintings. Monet's railway station is an iron-and-glass temple of steam, a cathedral of engineering and technology. Monet's locomotives are quite recognizable to the railway historian and enthusiast, from his little suburban *Tortillard* tank engine in the snow to the characteristic *pot de moutarde* ('mustard pot') express engine of the Chemin de fer de l'Ouest, nicknamed for its distinctive steam dome.

Eight of the Gare St. Lazare paintings were shown in 1877 at the third Impressionist exhibition (by this time, the Impressionists had accepted their nickname). The new organizer was Gustave Caillebotte (1848–93), who had stepped into the shoes of Bazille. Like Bazille, he was a man of independent means, but not at all an amateur. He was an accomplished painter in the realist tradition of Degas and Bazille rather than a true Impressionist, and his work featured solid, monumental figures in everyday settings. At the exhibition, he showed a view of the Pont de l'Europe, but in his composition the bridge is almost deserted, with only a couple and a stray dog, and there is no hint of the railway.

Monet showed 30 pictures altogether in the 1877 exhibition. Among them was the study of streets of Paris bunting bedecked to celebrate the opening of the International Exhibition: the *Rue Montorgueil Decked Out with Flags (La Rue Montorgueil: fête du 30 juin 1878).* Thin brush strokes of paint fluttering in all directions attempt to convey the movements of the blue, white and red flags above

Left: J.M.W. Turner. *Rain, Steam and Speed. The Great Western Railway*
1844 Oil on canvas
90.8 × 121.9 cm (35$^{3}/_{4}$ × 48 in)
National Gallery, London
Between the late works of Turner and the Impressionists there is a watershed. Although the setting of Rain, Steam and Speed *is recognizably Brunel's elliptically arched Maidenhead Bridge, with a 'Firefly' class locomotive, the scene is mythic, with its open wagons packed with travellers, the draperied figures waving, the hare running between the rails, the ploughman on the headland: the details are Ovidian.*

Right: *La rue Montorgueil, fête du 30 juin*
1878 Oil on canvas
81 × 50 cm (31$^{7}/_{8}$ × 19$^{5}/_{8}$ in)
Musée d'Orsay, Paris
Monet constantly changed his brushwork to match his subject, trying to find the physical equivalent in paint of flower petals, foliage, water, stone, drapery, and here, the flutter of tri-colour flags of the Republic en fête *in the streets of Paris.*

the surging crowds against the background of a canyon of ochreous stone buildings.

To his contemporaries, Monet must have seemed inconsistent, particularly when his paintings were seen for the first time: the Argenteuil boating scenes influenced by Renoir; the Argenteuil landscape, conventional tonal studies that might have been painted by Corot or Sisley; the widely differing Gare St. Lazare scenes; the Parasol pictures; the Parisian townscapes. All seem to be the work of a painter who cannot make up his mind. Every one is professionally competent, so they could not have been produced by an eclectic amateur thrashing about in a search for a technical method or an aesthetic identity. Nor are the pictures experimental steps into the unknown, for each in its individual way is brought to a satisfactory conclusion. The answer might lie in the fact that a painting by Monet carries all its qualities in its surface. This surface, the final statement, is completely tied to the subject. Thus they will vary as the subject varies, and will give a superficial impression that Monet was inconstant and inconsistent.

There is a very real sense in which Monet was self-taught. Whatever he had learned from his masters or his colleagues, and his range encompassed set-piece Academic portraits and the most experimental atmospheric paintings, he always seemed to find himself. He had to find the necessary means of expression in the process and progress of the work itself. In the true sense of the term, Monet remained a perpetual student. Each painting or series of paintings was an original challenge all over again. When every painting is, to a certain extent, an experiment, there must always be a degree of uncertainty. Painting in this way, attempting the impossible and always risking failure rather than contentedly exploring a well-tried formula must put a great

Above: *The Tuileries*
1876 Oil on canvas
53 x 72 cm (20⅞ x 28⅜ in)
Musée Marmottan, Paris
One of Monet's comparatively rare townscapes, the touch and texture of paint constantly varies to imply quite detailed foreground tree tops with strong, dark accents to throw foliage into three-dimensional relief.

Right: *Vase of Flowers*
*c.*1882 Oil on canvas
100 x 81 cm (39⅜ x 31⅞ in)
Courtauld Institute Galleries, London
Monet's flower paintings were without doubt painted as room centrepieces with an eye to the rich middle-class market. He used them to display virtuoso brushwork in rich variety.

personal strain upon the painter and affect his temperament.

Although painting is a social act in that a painter works for his time and for posterity, the act of painting is a solitary, often painful process, undertaken as a kind of compulsion. It is haunted by failure, not merely in the art market, but by the painter's own personal standards, and he is alone in being acutely aware of the gap between intention and achievement.

To his contemporaries, Monet certainly seemed to have his full share of artistic temperament. He spent money freely at Argenteuil, living in some style as he thought was his due, yet still sending, alternatively, abusive and begging letters to those friends trying to help him. He reacted angrily when they gave him practical advice on managing his affairs. In a good year, his income from his dealers and patrons could be 20,000 francs, ten times the average income of a working man with a family, and yet he would still be threatened with the bailiffs for bills of a few hundred francs. This erratic way of life is of a piece with the fierce way that Monet drove himself in his work.

The crash came in 1877. Monet's friend and patron Ernest Hoschedé, Belgian owner of a large Parisian department store, went bankrupt through mismanagement. He fled to Brussels to escape his creditors, leaving behind his young family and his wife, to whom Monet was very close. To pay his debts, his collection of pictures was sold at auction: Monets fetched from 50 to 500 francs, Renoirs went for 40, 50 and 80 francs, and a Pissarro was knocked down for 10 francs only. The whole market was affected. The art dealer Durand-Ruel found himself with a large stock of paintings on his hands that he would have to keep until the market recovered; in the meantime, he suffered from cash-flow problems. The Monet and Hoschedé families joined together for survival.

Opposite: *Monet's Garden at Vétheuil*
Dated 1880 Oil on canvas
150 × 120 cm (59 × 47¼ in)
National Gallery of Art, Washington D.C. Ailsa Mellon Bruce Collection

Below: *Vétheuil*
*c.*1880 Oil on canvas
59.7 × 80 cm (23½ × 31½ in)
Glasgow City Art Gallery, Glasgow

In September 1879, Camille died. Monet was forced to write to the family friend and physician Dr. de Bellio asking for money to redeem a pawned medallion of Camille's so that it could be buried with her. The artist also tried to sell pictures to the collector Victor Choquet for 40 or 50 francs. Manet tried to raise a fund among their friends to buy Monet's work for 1000 francs, but there was no response and, in the end, he did so from his own pocket. The magnificent *Gare St. Lazare* from the 1877 exhibition was sold to Dr. de Bellio for 64 francs.

Monet had already left Argenteuil for Vétheuil, north-west of Paris, where he painted the frozen Seine, chopping holes in the ice to set up his easel. In 1880, he determined to submit works to the Salon, which was beginning to modify its attitude towards Manet and Renoir. In doing so, he quarrelled with Degas and the hard core of Impressionists, and did not exhibit with the group

Melting Ice on the River Seine
1881 Oil on canvas
59 × 98.5 cm ($23^{1}/_{5}$ × $38^{3}/_{4}$ in)
Sammlung Oskar Reinhart Am Römmerholz, Winterthur
One of a series of canvases of this subject all made from sketches on the spot during a few hours in January 1880. Monet was proud of his fortitude in working under extreme conditions, standing frozen in snow and slush, or soaked by incoming waves on the seashore.

in 1880. Younger painters were coming along, and Monet inevitably found himself becoming one of the old guard. He sourly remarked that 'the little clique has become a great club which opens its doors to the first-come dauber.'

Following Camille's death, Alice Hoschedé was left with eight children and Monet to look after. Always searching for somewhere cheap to live in the suburbs of Paris, they moved from Vétheuil to Poissy, which Monet hated. Somehow they managed to survive, living from hand to mouth. Durand-Ruel, although himself in great financial difficulties throughout the 1880s, tried to do what he could for his painters. The art market being at a low ebb in Paris, he tried to find a public in London, but with no success. Then, like a miracle, so suddenly and coincidentally that it would be beyond belief in a work of fiction, the Americans came to the rescue. Here were the bourgeois, moneyed clients free from prejudice

Left: *The Flower Garden*
1886 Oil on canvas
65 × 54 cm (25$^{3}/_{5}$ × 21$^{1}/_{4}$ in)
Musée d'Orsay, Paris
Monet's garden at Giverny became a byword, but all his life, whatever his financial circumstances and wherever he lived, Monet's garden was a major part of his world. Flowers were as necessary to him as the basic staples of life.

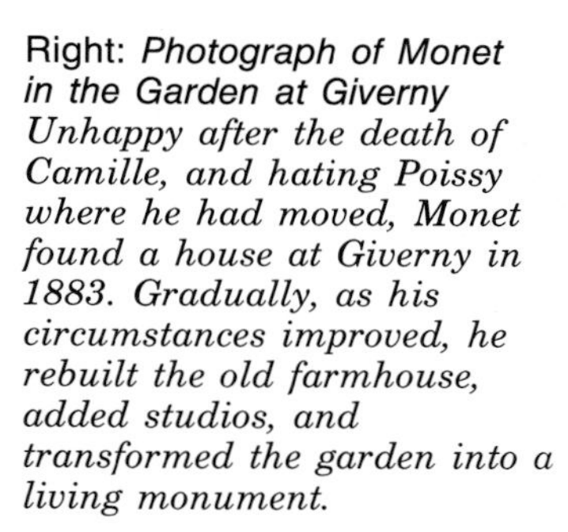

Right: *Photograph of Monet in the Garden at Giverny*
Unhappy after the death of Camille, and hating Poissy where he had moved, Monet found a house at Giverny in 1883. Gradually, as his circumstances improved, he rebuilt the old farmhouse, added studios, and transformed the garden into a living monument.

and willing to learn about and patronize modern painting. Durand-Ruel found himself suddenly having to compete with other dealers for the American market and for works to sell there. At first, the painters themselves were prejudiced and highly suspicious, but the new market was their salvation, and encouraged buyers in London, Berlin and even Moscow to follow suit.

In April 1883, Monet took the train from Poissy to Vernon. The lease had expired on the Poissy house, and Monet was delighted at the prospect of leaving it, even though he had nowhere to go. On the railway through the Epte valley, he discovered Giverny and found a house there. It was large but unpretentious, with no architectural features of any merit. It had a barn at either end for conversion into studios, and a large garden which was bordered by water meadows and the confluence of the Epte and the Seine where Monet could keep his boats: the floating studio, a rowing dinghy and two skiffs. It took ten days to move the household, the studio and the boats. Durand-Ruel advanced money to pay for the move.

The villagers expected Monet to be a free-handed incomer, living the life of the village squire; to them, he did not apparently have to work, but indulged himself in a hobby. However, Monet was not only perpetually short of money but tight-fisted outside his immediate circle. The peasants complained that he was painting *their* grain stacks and *their* poplar trees without payment or permission, and threatened to tear the stacks down and fell the trees, merely to annoy him.

The move to Giverny coincided with the death of Manet. Monet was a pall bearer at the funeral. Manet had become *hors concours* at the Salon and a Chevalier de la Légion d'honneur, a success that was 20 years too late. In 1899, hearing both that Manet's *Olympia* was up for sale and in danger of leaving the country, and that Manet's widow was in financial difficulties, Monet organized an appeal to buy the picture for the nation. The success of that appeal testifies to Monet's standing among collectors and fellow artists, even those of the Salon, and to the fact that he was succeeding Manet as the doyen of the movement.

In 1890, when Monet was 50, the freehold of Giverny became his. Two years later, when Hoschedé died in Belgium, Monet and Alice were married. It would appear that Monet had finally settled down to enjoy a secure middle age, living in the comfort which he always enjoyed, painting for a secure market, and spending a small fortune on his garden. He bought an adjacent plot of land, separated from his garden by a working railway line, and through which ran a stream. He built a sluice and gates and formed a large pond and water garden with a Japanese bridge. He employed six gardeners and became intensely interested in horticulture, propagating, crossing and hybridizing flowers; he also had a large greenhouse of exotics including rare orchids. The village *abbé*, who was a keen botanist, became a close family friend.

Somewhat to Monet's distress, but much to the villagers' delight, Giverny was invaded by Americans in their new enthusiasm for modern French painting. They converted lofts and barns

into studios and paid inflated prices for everything. Giverny became an artists' colony, and students hung about hoping for a glimpse of Monet at work.

At Giverny, Monet established a working habit of rising before dawn and going to the site of his motif to capture the effects of the earliest light. He worked through daybreak and dawn until the sun was up. By late morning, he would be back in his studio or with his gardeners until lunch, which was always punctual. This was followed by rest until late afternoon, when he would again study the changing light at the close of day. If work went well and the light was good, Monet was hospitable and expansive, to Alice's great relief. If he was dissatisfied or the weather turned bad, he was sulky and morose, and would retire to bed.

Monet's routine is hardly that of a temperamental genius waiting for inspiration to strike and then working in a frenzy. It is more the work-pattern of a country craftsman, dependent upon the weather, getting his task done while he can in a methodical manner. Monet was rather proud of this, and liked to affect a blunt, workman-like attitude to his painting. He even dressed the part. When working along the Normandy coast, which he continued to do every year, he donned fisherman's oilskins, sou'wester and high boots. In the country, he looked like a sportsman out for a day's rough shooting across the stubble, wearing a large shooter's coat with poachers pockets, shooting breeches and puttees or gaiters, with a broad-brimmed sportsman's hat.

Above: *The Cliffs at Etretât*
1885 Oil on canvas
65 x 81 cm (25 3/5 x 31 7/8 in)
Sterling and Francine Clark Art Institute, Williamstown, Massachusetts
The cliffs at Etretât were another recurring theme.

Right: *Lavacourt Under Snow*
1881 Oil on canvas
59.7 x 80 cm (23 1/2 x 31 1/2 in)
National Gallery, London. On loan to the Hugh Lane Municipal Gallery of Modern Art, Dublin
Painted at Vétheuil during the same winter that he made studies of ice floes in the river from his floating studio.

Working out of doors became more than an act of study; it became an act of faith. He loved to tell an audience how tough one had to be, like a countryman or man of the sea. For example, while working at the very edge of the sea, a giant wave swept all his equipment away and nearly drowned him; he escaped by climbing a steep cliff at an even greater risk to his life. Like Turner, who also loved to encourage such stories, he tied himself to a bench on the deck of a ship to witness

a storm at sea. Friends told of Monet coming in from a winter's day of painting frozen stiff, his coat and trousers like boards, his beard and hair a mass of icicles. Degas related an anecdote of Monet at Varengeville, near Dieppe: Monet arrived with all his impedimenta, looked at the sky and shouted, 'Half an hour too late! I shall have to come back tomorrow!'

To his colleagues Manet and Degas, Monet's fetish of painting on the spot had become something of a joke. 'Painting is not an outdoor sport,' they said. There is no doubt a degree of exaggeration in Monet's tales, but he was not the first nor the last to over-emphasize the physical difficulties faced by the artist. The layman's view of the painter as a self-indulgent *bon vivant* living comfortably off the accident of talent is enough to provoke any serious artist into hyperbolic defence.

The American, John Singer Sargent (1856–1925), who became a fashionable portrait painter in London and New York, was a regular visitor to the Monet house and painted Monet at his easel. Sargent took over the leadership of the Americans in Paris from James McNeill Whistler (1834–1903). 'One Sargent does not make an

John Singer Sargent. *Claude Monet Painting at the Edge of a Wood*
*c.*1887 Oil on canvas
54 × 64.8 cm (21½ × 25½ in)
Tate Gallery, London
The American painter Sargent painted Monet at work in his floating studio, and here, with Blanche Hoschédé sitting by, in a meadow behind the house at Giverny. Sargent even shows us the subject 'laid in' on Monet's canvas. Ultimately Monet felt himself persecuted by would-be followers coming to Giverny, particularly compatriots of Sargent's, although one of them became his stepson-in-law.

army,' said Whistler. 'Nor does one Whistler make an orchestra,' replied Sargent. He also introduced the young American painter Theodore Butler to the family. After some opposition, Butler married a Hoschedé daughter, Suzanne, but she died young in 1899. Alice was inconsolable.

Partly as a distraction, Monet bought a motor car, a Panhard Lavassor, and his studio handyman became chauffeur. The purchase was a great success. All the Monets and Hoschedés became speed mad, and Monet as owner, not driver, was taken to court. They followed motor rallies and races, and the cycle races. The two sons bought cars as soon as they were old enough, and then the whole family would set off in convoy for expeditions to the sea, for picnics or to try restaurants and hotels. Monet had himself driven to see the Soeurs Tatin at their kitchen to settle an argument about their apple tart, and to Madrid to see the works of Velasquez in the Prado museum.

The house and garden at Giverny became a fashionable place of pilgrimage. The famous competed for introductions and invitations, to have lunch in the famous yellow dining room, to be photographed in the garden and, more rarely, to be allowed into a studio.

Monet kept up with his friends Renoir and Pissarro, but as they grew older, the painters tended to stay at home, concentrating on their work. Renoir, increasingly disabled with arthritis after a bicycling accident, moved to Cagnes-sur-Mer and the sunshine of the South of France. Pissarro, whose eyesight was failing, was either in Paris or with his family in London.

Cézanne made a memorable visit to Giverny. He stayed at the Hôtel Baudry (once a village inn and now patronized by artists and their friends) and painted locally. He and Monet exchanged paintings, a great mutual compliment between two equally touchy, difficult men. At a lunch party, they were joined by the art critic Claude Geffroy and Georges Clemenceau, who in the French tradition combined the professions of politician and man of letters, and for whose newspaper *La Justice* Geffroy wrote. Clemenceau was to play an important part in Monet's later life. Also at the table was Auguste Rodin, with whom Monet had just shared a very successful exhibition in Paris.

Perhaps not without a touch of malice, Cézanne announced to the guests that 'Monsieur Rodin [who had been awarded the Légion d'honneur] isn't at all proud – he shook hands with me!' Later in the garden, he amazed them all by kneeling before Rodin and thanking him. Next day, while lunching at Monet's table with Renoir and Sisley, Cézanne took it into his head that they were patronizing him when they praised his painting. He abruptly got up from the table and left Giverny, leaving his pictures behind at the hotel. Monet

Left: *Monet in his Studio at Giverny*
The walls of Monet's studios were hung with pictures crowded edge to edge in haphazard order, framed and unframed. He would intermittently work at the easel, at his desk, or simply look at pictures for hours.

Right: *The Church at Varangeville*
1882 Oil on canvas
65 x 81 cm ($25^{3}/_{5}$ x $31^{7}/_{8}$ in)
Barber Institute of Fine Arts, University of Birmingham
The small church on the headland not far from Dieppe was painted towards sunset. Heavily reworked in the studio, the canvas is scarred with looping scratches made with the pointed handle of Monet's brush to convey the wiry branches of the pines and gorse. Seemingly arbitary accents of bright scarlet give glitter to the middle and foreground. The modern painter Georges Braque is buried here.

carefully forwarded the canvases to Cézanne, who thanked him. They never met again.

Monet was not mellowed by age. He became a domestic tyrant whose moods affected the whole household. His obsession for perfection coupled with his declared intention of painting the impossible caused him to have sudden doubts about finished work, which he would seize and spoil by scraping and repainting in the most brutal way, and then destroy. He became increasingly reluctant to let paintings go, playing off dealers one against the other, pushing up prices, and then calling the deal off altogether. Even the loyal Durand-Ruel was made to suffer.

In the studio which doubled as his sitting room and study, Monet hung his own works, frame to frame, three deep on the wall, where he would sit looking at them, changing and re-hanging. Elsewhere throughout the house he had hanging 13 Cézannes, nine Renoirs, three Pissarros, three Delacroix, two Signacs (surprisingly, one of Monet's young 'daubers'), pictures by Fantin-Latour, Degas, Sisley, Berthe Morisot and Caillebotte and two Rodin bronzes. He also owned a superb collection of Japanese prints, and with them hung a framed Lautrec poster of Yvette Guilberte.

The kitchen was a haze of blue-and-white tiling and two-toned blue paint, and the yellow dining room, also in two tones, had chairs painted to match and a specially made china service. Japanese prints hung on the walls, and in fine weather Monet had the large glass doors open. His seat at table faced the main axis of the garden, off which he never took his eyes, drinking in each moment.

Right: *Monet and Gustave Geffroy.* Photographed by Sacha Guitry
An invitation to Giverny was a great honour. The critic Geffroy was a regular visitor, And so were the actor Sacha Guitry and his actress wife Charlotte Lyses. Visits were usually recorded with a photograph during a walk round the garden.

The Series

There is a sense in which Monet always painted series of pictures. The early tonal pictures, the picnic and garden subjects, the Argenteuil riverside paintings, the Parisian street scenes and, above all, the Gare St. Lazare paintings – all form related groups in which the individual pictures together make a recognizable sequence. The Gare St. Lazare studies are related by subject matter, by the setting and by the objective – the rendering of light, air, vapours and movement – and the sketches and worked-up pictures, made on the spot, all build up towards the great studio masterpiece.

Monet himself, and the critics, used the word 'series' to describe sets of canvases being worked on simultaneously and serially on the same subject or theme. However, it might be better to save the specific term 'series' for strongly related works which have a clear objective beyond their individual identities, with usually a foundation or starting point which is theoretical, and which, together, form a related whole. Pictures more loosely related by shared subject matter could be said to form 'groups'.

Monet's series all date from the time of the move to Giverny onwards. It was probably the new-found sense of security and stability that enabled the artist to turn his back on the market for a while and virtually become a student again. The subject matter was at his own doorstep. The spring and summer of 1890 saw Monet at work on two of the series: the Grain Stacks and the Poplars. The grain stacks, or cornricks, could be seen from the windows of the house. The poplars were just across the fields where the Epte joined the Seine.

Le bassin aux nymphéas. Harmonie rose
1900 Oil on canvas
89 × 100 cm (35 × 39 3/8 in)
Musée d'Orsay, Paris
Monet told Geffroy, 'I planted my water-lilies for fun, when I saw, all of a sudden, that my pond had become enchanted. I seized my palette. Since then I have had no other model'. In 1909 he exhibited 48 large canvases of the lily pond, with and without the Japanese bridge with its wisteria. The exhibition was a complete success.

The Grain Stacks

There are more than 30 paintings of the grain stacks, all closely related variations on a theme. The views are taken from this angle and that, advancing to close-up, then retreating to mid- and long shot, as if Monet were experimenting with a camera lens. In fact, he had become a keen photographer and student of photography at Giverny, constantly keeping a picture record of his garden through the changing seasons. Now he was apparently trying to turn himself into a camera, with all the implications of scientific objectivity.

Monet seemed to underestimate what he had begun when he started his series. He told the Duc de Trevise, 'I first of all believed that two canvases would do, one for grey weather and one for the sun. One day I saw that the light had changed. I asked my step-daughter to fetch another canvas, then another; still another. I worked on each one only when I had my effect . . . The sun sets so fast that I cannot follow it,' he lamented. 'I work so slowly that I am desperate . . . the more I continue, the more I see . . . More than ever I am dissatisfied with things that come easily, in one stroke.'

He worked on up to seven canvases at a time, dashing from one to the other as the light changed. A minute or so from the house, and he could be face to face with his subject. Even more important was the fact that he would beat a hasty retreat with his work to the shelter of the studio in wind or rain – no climbing up cliffs with everything on his back.

Referring to St. Denis, patron saint of France, who reputedly walked after his beheading from Montmartre to the site of his chapel, Madame du Deffand remarked, 'It's the first step that counts.' She might have said, if she had been born a century later, that in Monet's case it is the last touch that counts.

However much work was done in the open air, it is reasonable to assume that the finishing touch was carried out in the studio, with the canvases side by side, and the painter considering them without distraction, taking his time. For the painter must not only respond to what he sees on the spot, but even more, he must be aware of what the painting needs. Although the paintings in the Grain Stacks series are masterpieces in their own right, they are meant to be seen together, where they make more than the sum of the parts. Monet could only have ensured this by finishing them together, and that meant working in the studio. Even though Monet's constant retouching means that it is almost impossible to put the series into chronological order, although they do have seasonal identities, these

Grain Stacks. End of Summer. Morning
1891 Oil on canvas
60.5 × 100 cm ($23^{4}/_{5}$ × $39^{3}/_{8}$ in)
Musée d'Orsay, Paris
Monet worked on several canvases at a time in order to capture the changing light. The field with the grain stacks was immediately behind the house, visible from the windows. The painting of the whole grain stack series is very complex. Paint is applied both in successive layers and in carefully placed dabs of paint side by side (see details). The brush strokes no longer literally imitate the physical features in the landscape, straw, leaves and grass, but are subordinated to the effect or 'envelope' of light and cast shadow.

questions should not worry us or affect our enjoyment of these great works.

As a subject, the grain stacks would not seem to have enough substance to sustain an artist's interest over 30 paintings. They are not just ordinary, but banal to a degree. They were not sited with an eye to contrast with, say, a stream or a clump of trees. They were actually close to buildings, but the buildings never appear. It must be that Monet deliberately chose as unpromising and dead-pan a subject as possible, so that nothing could distract him (or the spectator of the finished result) from his stated objective, which was to record in paint, as accurately as possible, the same scene at various times of the day and in various states of weather.

Monet painted them as he found them, varying his viewpoint as he moved about, but not making any special effort to compose them on the canvas. In other works, he consciously manipulated his composition, not just by eliminating or rearranging features in the landscape, but by careful use of simple geometry on the picture plane – for example, in the Argenteuil paintings, in the diagonal stretch of a sailing boat's forestay, or the white patch of a sail, or the vertical cutting of the canvas by a mast. In the series, he turned himself into a neutral recorder, but this must be qualified. He was not a recorder of grain stacks, nor even a recorder of nature and the seasons. The latter would be invisible to the countryman, a day-to-day non-event, and unnoticeable to the townsman, who would not give a second glance. Any painter except Monet would have shrugged his shoulders and moved on. Yet the result of these canvases is that we are held, stopped in our tracks, by any one of them.

Monet made a general statement about his work: 'I was trying to do the impossible . . . to paint light itself.' He was semi-apologetic, semi-defiant. Never free from doubt, the impossible was his excuse. For us, it is a simple, positive statement. There was no subject. The stacks and fields were merely a medium, specimens for observation of a phenomenon. He painted the

Grain Stacks. Sunset. Frosty Weather
1891 Oil on canvas
69 × 92 cm (27 1/5 × 36 1/5 in)
Private collection
The series was worked upon side by side, in the studio, where the finishing overpaintings and retouches were applied, so that maximum contrast could be made between the blue haze of summer in bright light, and the musky warm brown light of winter. Details right: *The texture of the grain stack is as close and rich as a slice of dark plum pudding. Light*

blue, pink and yellow paint spattered across the ground give it a hard frosty look. The distant trees are blue and brown, with dark red-brown roofs seen under them.

stacks in the light and against the light, in early and late light, in blue mists and a warm orange glow, in a dry brown field, in a young, sprouting, green field, touched by a rime of hoar frost, sprinkled with snow.

This series is also about painting. These pictures were studies, we must remember, and Monet was studying, researching his already mature and competent technique. He was trying to match solid paint, fixed and intractable, with intangible, changing light. Through application of the paint to the canvas, the use of colour theory, carefully mixing calculated harmonics of tone and colour, matching synthetic arrangements of colour (which existed in his head, not in nature) to what he saw, he tried to evoke an image, not ultimately to paint reality, or to paint, but to create an illusion.

Previously Monet had tried to match the texture and form of his paint to the texture and form of natural objects. Rounded puffs of steam are imitated by the twirl of a brush, or fluttering strips of bunting by thin strokes of paint; dabs and touches of paint become leaves and grasses, or ripples of light and shade of water. His was a search for a visual equivalent of onomatopoeia in poetry. Even in the *Gare St. Lazare*, the paint still follows the forms it implies.

In the Grain Stacks series, the paint does not imitate. It is applied in dots and spots which become smaller and more precise as the picture progresses. He set the key of a picture as does a composer in music. Each study exploits a specific colour range of blue and orange, discordant and contrasting, or violet and green, closely harmonizing. Red-browns are built out of red, green and violet touches of paint. There are strange combinations of rose-pinks and apple-greens. His starting point is the colour theory that he had learned, but the work is that of a painter in full maturity setting down all that he knows about colour and exploring still further.

Monet did come once or twice close to the painting technique called 'Pointillism', or sometimes 'Divisionism', which was developed by the painter Georges Seurat (1859–91). He took to painting with tiny dots of pure colour, to mix 'optically' in the eye at normal viewing distance, to a logical, or extreme, conclusion. In Seurat's landscapes, all the greens on a lawn would be painted in varying proportions of blue and yellow dots, with red and violet dots in the shadows. Pissarro fell quite under the spell of the younger painter and took up Pointillism with enthusiasm, making, so they thought, a nuisance of himself to his old contemporaries. Monet, who had suffered in the artists' fight to have an essential element of freedom in their work accepted, seems to have thought Pointillism too mechanical, too much like painting to a formula, and objected to the works painted in this manner being included in the exhibition of 1886. However, he possessed paintings by Paul Signac who, as a follower of Seurat, was even more of a theoretician.

Cézanne said of Monet, 'He is only an eye, but what an eye!' This might imply that Monet was an intuitive, non-intellectual painter, but nothing is further from the truth. Monet's work is as cerebrally disciplined as, say, a set of musical variations upon a simple theme, while it maintains that improvisatory illusion that is the hallmark of the truly great artist. We accept these contrived, calculated, synthetic images as if they have grown spontaneously out of the soil.

Grain Stacks. Snow Effect. Sunshine
1891 Oil on canvas
64.8 × 92.1 cm (25½ × 36¼ in)
National Gallery of Scotland, Edinburgh
The dark grain stacks throw a bright blue shadow across the white and gold ground. Thirty pictures of the grain stacks are known. Either of one or two stacks, Monet slightly varied both the view and his distance from them. Having started them on the spot, he finished them in groups in the studio. 'I need a moment of peace and quiet before I can put finishing touches to them', he said.

Details left: *The complex method of painting takes us back to the finished* Gare St. Lazare. *Surprisingly, after all the earlier difficulties, the* Grain Stacks *were a great success. The least promising of subjects, they lent themselves to transformation to the utmost degree.*

The Cliffs at Fécamp
1881 Oil on canvas
63.5 × 80 cm (25 × 31½ in)
Aberdeen Art Gallery and Musuem, Aberdeen
At Fécamp and Dieppe Monet worked on the cliff tops. In this painting the tide is in, washing the foot of the cliff with no beach visible. The expanse is unbroken to the horizon, while the distinct planes of the cliff top recede in a rhythmic progression. Clouds, waves and grasses are painted with innumerable light touches of colour, approaching a pointillist technique.

The Poplars

The series of grain stacks were overlapped by the Poplars series. The river Epte, a tributary of the Seine on its north bank, marked the boundary between two *départements*, the Ile de France and Normandy, placing Giverny just inside the latter. Monet kept his boats moored at the confluence of the two rivers, and walked across the water meadows at daybreak to work in his studio boat. The poplars lined the bank of the Epte and turned along the Seine.

The Poplars are more broadly painted than the Grain Stacks, as if in relief from the tight, painstaking precision of the 'dots'. This really does seem to reinforce the supposition that Monet looked upon the Grain Stacks

Below: *Poplars*
1891 Oil on canvas
90 x 93 cm (35 2/5 x 36 3/5 in)
Fitzwilliam Museum, Cambridge
In this dramatic composition the poplars follow the curve of the river bank swinging into the centre of the picture, back to the left and then down and away to the right. Cropping heightens the rhythm and space.

Right: *Poplars on the Epte*
1891 Oil on canvas
92.4 x 73.7 cm (36 3/8 x 29 in)
Tate Gallery, London
The composition is poster-like, with both the foreground and the tree tops cropped, as is the apex of the reverse curve of the line of trees on the left of the picture. The paint is broadly handled and has the appearance of being entirely painted on the spot, but in fact it was retouched and finished in the studio.

as a literal study, not merely in the artist's loose sense of the word. Now, in the Poplars, swirling brush strokes delineate tumbling clouds. The tree trunks are firmly drawn in long brush strokes, not built up from dots and dabs. The trees are carefully arranged in vertical bars across the canvas, the intervals between them carefully chosen. There is evidence that Monet changed them fractionally in the pictures before making his final decision. There is conscious picture-making here, not subordination to the subject as found.

The poplars are painted with the light and against the light. The timescale of the series is from summer through autumn to winter, not the whole year round as in the first series. The colours are deliberately schematic, as all Monet's work would be from now on, but much simpler in range than the grain stacks series. They are all much lighter in tone, with a great deal of white used with the colours: green and gold, green and blue, with soft violet-browns and violet-greys. The forms are starkly dramatic, almost poster-like.

Rather surprisingly in view of the state of the art market, both series were a commercial success when shown in Paris. Fifteen of the grain stack pictures were exhibited in 1891, hung in three groups of five to emphasize their close relationship. Pissarro complained that people talked of nothing else.

Poplars on the Epte
1891 Oil on canvas
81.9 x 81.3 cm (32¼ x 32 in)
National Gallery of Scotland, Edinburgh
The poplars on the river Epte, a brook-like tributary of the Seine, were grown as a crop by the farmer. Monet found them already marked for felling but persuaded the farmer to stay his hand.

Below: *Detail of tree trunks and riverbank in the centre right of the painting.*

Rouen Cathedral

When the news was heard that Monet was painting a similar series of Rouen Cathedral, offers came in to buy them sight unseen. This series, painted between 1892 and 1894, posed peculiar problems for the painter and for the spectator. First of all, the site is extremely restricted. Unlike the great square in front of Notre-Dame in Paris, the rectangular space in front of Rouen Cathedral is rather cramped and narrow and, in Monet's time, was cluttered with market stalls. Today it is full of motor cars, and the tourist, dodging traffic, has to crane his neck to see the façade, either looking at the porch or up at the towers; it is difficult to do both at once. Even when Monet was painting, the square could hardly have been a suitable place in which to set up easel, paint boxes, canvases, stool and umbrella, to settle down to uninterrupted, concentrated study. Biographers say that Monet painted from a first-floor window opposite the cathedral. Monet's series reflects the awkwardness of the site; the façade is cut top and bottom, and is sharply angled and cut at the right.

Given enough elbow room, a painter can rearrange what he sees on site when he composes on his canvas. He may have to look down at his feet, then up at the sky, from right to left and back, constantly changing his viewpoint but settling everything to a uniform scheme on the canvas as if able mentally to step back to unify the view. Monet usually did this in his work, editing and selecting both in his landscapes and townscapes, both at ground level and from upper windows. Here he was stuck in close up, nose to subject as if dictated to by inescapable circumstances.

The motif – that is, the visual theme – is as hard and unyielding as the stone of which the cathedral façade is built. Flowers in a vase, or objects in a still life, can be rearranged. No one is going to say, 'But it was not like that.' Landscapes are selected. Even sitters' poses can be changed in a portrait, and distortions made without much argument. But architecture is there for everyone to see. Each Gothic church is quite specific. That is Amiens, that is Chartres and this is Rouen. Each has its own peculiarities, in form, proportion and detail, particularly in close-up. There can be no varying of the motif here, and one is struck by the almost identical similarity of composition of the whole series of pictures. 'Not enough sky, not enough ground' was the critics' comment. Paul Signac said, 'I fully understand what these cathedrals are: marvellously executed walls.'

The sole variations are of effects of light upon the stone façade at various times of the

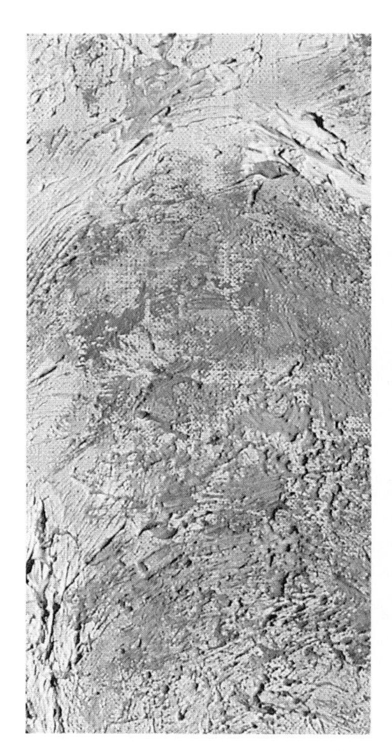

Left: *Rouen Cathedral. Morning Sunlight. Harmony in Blue*
1893 – 94 Oil on canvas
91 × 63 cm (35⁴/₅ × 24⁴/₅ in)
Musée d'Orsay, Paris
The detail at top shows the arch above the main door to the cathedral.

Rouen Cathedral. West Façade. Sunlight
1894 Oil on canvas
100 × 66 cm (39³/₈ × 26 in)
National Gallery of Art, Washington D.C. Chester Dale Collection
The detail above clearly shows the effect of impasto.

Rouen Cathedral. Façade in Sunlight
Undated Oil on canvas
104 x 73.6 cm (41 x 29 in)
Sterling and Francine Clark Art Institute, Williamstown, Massachussetts

day and in various types of weather. There is no distraction from Monet's purpose. The unvarying monotony of the theme underlines the subtle changes of tone and colour from one picture to the next. To give a musical analogy, the theme of Beethoven's Diabelli variations is a little waltz tune that is banal to the point of mental torture, but in the master's hands, it produced perhaps the greatest example of the genre. It is the same with Monet's themes and variations: the grain stacks, the poplars, Rouen Cathedral. Once stated, the simplest theme is merely a starting point, a peg to hang the idea on. Perhaps in the Rouen series, eye, paint, brain and image can go no further. Paint is executed in layer upon layer until not only the subject, the stone façade, appears to be in danger of dissolving, melting, but the paint itself seems about to run, drip and fall off the canvas, collapsing into a uniform grey mass. In his search for form and colour, Monet comes perilously close to destroying both.

There is a strong sense that the Rouen series is close-ended. If any of Monet's works could be called absolutely finished, allowing for no change or alteration, both individually and as a series, it is this series. Thus these pictures form a climax in his work. However, Monet was an explorer, voyaging into the unknown, and exploration must be open-ended, not closed. For him, such voyages, often painfully and unwillingly undertaken, were not over.

The Rouen series seemed to coincide with a crisis in Impressionism itself. The members of the group were moving apart, and the aims that they had held in common – the free expression of their simple themes – were no longer adequate. If in the Rouen series it seems as if Impressionism can go no further, so Monet's colleagues seemed to have reached the limits in their own work.

Manet, never a true Impressionist, had died in 1883 and, in any case, had always held himself aloof from the group, as had Degas and Toulouse-Lautrec. Camille Pissarro, on the verge of security and success with a market for his paintings, perversely turned his back on his achievements in a search for perpetual change, and took up the cause of Pointillism. Renoir abandoned Impressionism for a new classicism, turning to Rubens for themes and technique, bringing both up to date in the 20th century. Cézanne, who under Pissarro's guidance had evolved from making painfully clumsy attempts at Baroque painting to become a competent Impressionist, was not content to remain so. Instead, he became increasingly analytical and highly structured in his work, his geometric forms standing out in clear distinction from each other and pointing the way to Cubism.

The younger painters, Paul Gauguin and Vincent Van Gogh, were already becoming known as Post-Impressionists. Although both had worked as Impressionists for a short while, their highly idiosyncratic styles of painting opened new prospects of personal expression for their successors.

The first generation had moved on, into the highly individual final phases of their work. The second generation of their pupils and followers were re-interpreting the Impressionist ideas and practices. Save for Monet. Modern hindsight shows him to have held firmly to his original course to the end.

Rouen Cathedral. West Façade
1894 Oil on canvas
100 x 66cm (39 3/8 x 26 in)
National Gallery of Art, Washington D.C. Chester Dale Collection
Monet spoke of the difficulties encountered in trying to finish his pictures away from the subject. It has been said that he tried to match the texture of the old stones with encrusted paint (see detail) but the light and shade in paint is like a corrosive fluid that eats the stone away. The whole picture seems on the point of melting and dissolving.

Monet's London

During his Giverny years, Monet made several trips abroad. One, surprisingly, was to Norway in 1895, a journey perhaps more significant for the long, autobiographical statement that he gave to the poet Henri Bang, with whom he stayed, than from any exceptional work that he did there. In 1900, he made a painting trip to Venice, where he and Sargent stayed at the same hotel, and in 1905, he was driven all the way to the Prado museum in Madrid to look at the Velasquez paintings.

Monet retained an affection for London and visited it often – surprisingly, perhaps, in view of the indifferent, if not hostile, reception accorded him on his first visit as a penniless war refugee in 1870. He had established friendships with Whistler and Sargent in Paris, and spent two weeks in London in 1887 as Whistler's guest. He returned to London the following year and again in 1891, 1898, 1899 and 1900. He showed work in mixed exhibitions, at the New English Art Club, at the Royal Society of British Artists when Whistler was president, and at the Goupil Gallery's London Impressionists show in December 1889. His last trip to London was in 1901.

London is not an obviously beautiful city. It has its monuments but they are scattered and tucked away, and have to be sought out by the tourist; there are no splendid vistas and avenues. The London of Monet's day was a busy industrial town with chemical works, foundries and lead mills. It was a busy sea port, and shipbuilding was still important. It was grimy, and London fogs – a lethal mixture of water vapour like a suspended rainfall and coal smoke, corroding sulphur and other fumes – were legendary. Neither was it a friendly city. There was no café life; the citizens were xenophobic and not very well disposed to each other, either. One wonders why any Parisian would want to leave his native city for such a grim, uncivilized place.

Yet London had its strange attractions. Political refugees from all over Europe found a freedom in its indifference. It was this that attracted Verlaine and Rimbaud, and was celebrated in a poem about London in the latter's *Les Illuminations* (1886). Through a yellow fog thickened by opium fumes, Rimbaud's burly figures loom silently, menacingly, intent upon some personal crime. Their eyes shine yellow like locomotive lamps, their teeth gleam like steel guillotines. Tram cars are swaying chalets of wood and glass lit by blue flashes of lightning.

In his illustrated *London*, Gustave Doré drew dockworkers and brewers' draymen, and his engraving of the Retort house in Brick Lane in the East End is like a scene in Hell. He also illustrated Dante's *Inferno*, and his London is quite as fantastic and as sinister, even though Mansion House station on the District Line is quite recognizable. Even his scenes of high-life are full of hidden violence.

Des Esseintes, the perverted and self-centred hero of J.K. Huysmans' *A Rebours*, was fascinated by these accounts of London, and set out to see the city for himself. On his way to the Gare du Nord to catch the night train for the Channel crossing, he picked up an English newspaper and ordered steak and kidney pudding and porter in the Parisian version of an English pub. Going out into a foggy,

Below left: Gustave Doré.
Inside London Docks from *London, a Pilgrimage*
1872 Engraving
Doré came to London in 1869 at the invitation of the radical journalist William Blanchard Jerrold. They found the dockland and East End slums romantic, picturesque and excitingly dangerous.

Left: Gustave Doré. *Lambeth Gas Works* from *London a Pilgrimage*
1872 Engraving
This illustration is further dramatized by the florid engraving which typifies Doré's work.

Above: *London. The Houses of Parliament. Sunshine Through the Fog*
1904 Oil on canvas
81 × 92 cm (32 × 36$^{1}/_{5}$ in)
Musée d'Orsay, Paris
The Houses of Parliament revealed by the sun shining through the fog is seen across the Thames from the south bank on the site of St. Thomas's Hospital. Monet says that here he had up to 100 canvases on the go. He would return to the same canvas over and over again.

Above: *London. The Houses of Parliament. Sunset*
1903 Oil on canvas
81.3 x 92.5 cm (32 x 36²/₅ in)
National Gallery of Art, Washington D.C. Chester Dale Collection
Monet changed his technique again in London, matching mist and fog in thin fluid paint in translucent layers, then accenting highlights in touches of impasto paint.

Opposite top: *The Thames at Charing Cross*
1903 Oil on canvas
73.5 x 100.5 cm (29 x 39½ in)
Musée des Beaux Arts, Lyons
The railway bridge at Charing Cross is no beauty, but must have reminded Monet of the railway bridge at Argenteuil to which it is so similar in structure. Monet painted his views from rooms at the Savoy Hotel, then a family hotel.

drizzly night, he then decided that he had had the English experience without the disagreeable side-effects of a cross-Channel voyage, and returned home to bed.

This was every Frenchman's view of London, the counterpart of the Anglo-Saxon myth of the *gaieté parisienne*, and this is what excited Monet. During his visit to London in 1887, he stayed at the Grosvenor hotel, next to Victoria station, not venturing very far and close enough to Whistler in Chelsea. For his subsequent working visits, he stayed at the Savoy hotel on the Thames Embankment. In Monet's time, the Savoy was not the grand affair it is today, but a hotel in the French manner in a terrace of old houses. From his windows there, Monet could see both

Waterloo Bridge and the Charing Cross railway bridge (officially known as Hungerford Bridge), and he worked from his bedroom. For the Westminster views, further upstream, he worked from a room on the site of St. Thomas's Hospital opposite the Houses of Parliament.

Sargent visited Monet in his fifth-floor room at the Savoy in 1899, and saw canvases stacked six deep against all four walls. Monet would work on them one after another, setting the theme, subject, colour and tone, and then take them back to finish in the studio at Giverny. He was in London from February to April 1900, and from January to April 1901, each time staying at the Savoy. Contemporary accounts list at least 42 Waterloo Bridge pictures, 35 Charing Cross and 20 Houses of Parliament. The pictures seem to have been painted in that order, but a true chronology, or even consistent titling is now impossible to sort out and, in any case, rather pointless. Many of the pictures were worked and re-worked in the studio, some much more than others, but others were left in the same state as they were in London. All the paintings were exhibited and sold out of sequence, and the titles given to them were very much afterthoughts, distinguished one from another in exhibition catalogues by name as well as number.

They have their origin in the 1871 picture, *The Thames at Westminster* (*La Tamise et le Parlement*), painted in a direct, simple tonal style, very much after Manet. The scene is bathed in a yellowish-green light, with a landing stage in the foreground and the Palace of Westminster silhouetted in the fog, very much exaggerated vertically. The picture is very definite, very foursquare.

The technique of the later London pictures is very different. They are among the most atmospheric of all Monet's works. They are not built up in thick encrustations of paint like the grain stacks, the poplars or the Rouen pictures, but painted in thin translucent washes which imitate the mist and fog, with solid paint reserved for highlights. The technique is close to that which the Italian Renaissance painters called *sfumato*, or 'smoky'. Layers of paint are spread thinly over each other to form a milky, ambiguous haze. Here Monet approaches the English painter Turner in technique, and his most Turneresque picture is of Waterloo Bridge in a fog, signed and dated 1903 (at Giverny).

The Waterloo Bridge of that time was the elegant Rennie-designed structure of rusticated and pilastered arches stretching like a Renaissance arcade across the river (it was replaced in the 1930s by a severe but still elegant bridge). Charing Cross Bridge still stands as it was then, a girder bridge on squat columns very like the bridge at Argenteuil, a thing of no beauty until translated by a painter's vision. The neo-Gothic Houses of Parliament are equally as important as symbol and building, and Big Ben, the clock tower, means *London* as the Eiffel Tower means *Paris*.

Monet, recalling in 1920 the days when he was working on the London series, said that he had had up to 100 canvases on the go at the same time. He described searching frantically among them for the right one to match the scene at a particular moment. In haste and panic, he would seize on the one that most nearly approximated, alter it, ruin it and then, too late, the light having changed, find the right one after all. He would, he said, work and re-work a single painting up to 20 or 30 times as the circumstances demanded. And all this while working in a hotel room.

Allowing for a little exaggeration, there may have been 50 canvases rather than 100, and re-working might have involved a touch here and a touch there on a row of paintings placed side by side, as well as a great deal of just looking and thinking. When in London, Monet spent months at a stretch in single-minded concentration on his work, with very little socializing.

And then, back in the large studio at Giverny, with pastel drawings also made in London as reference, he would settle down to paint and re-paint: pictures that look absolutely as if painted on the spot are dated 1902 and 1903 when Monet was never in London. Durand-Ruel was constantly asking for the London pictures, but three years elapsed between Monet's last visit to London in 1901 and the 1904 exhibition in Paris of 37 of the paintings. Monet was insistent that canvases only left his studio when he considered them ready, whatever clients and dealers might think. He needed them all, round the studio, in order to work on any one.

There was to have been an exhibition of the series in London in 1905, the opening of which he would have attended, but disagreements with Durand-Ruel held it up.

Then Sargent said that Monet worked from photographs of the Houses of Parliament, and the French artist took this as a slur on his honesty and withdrew from the exhibition altogether.

As Monet's handling of paint constantly changed to match the qualities of atmosphere that he was trying to paint, so did his compositional ideas. The grain stacks are foursquare, framed by the canvas as he saw them. The poplar trees are sometimes topped and tailed, implying that the trees continue either side of and above and below the canvas, as if we are looking through an opening in a sheet of card to isolate one passage in a continuous scene – indeed, Monet may have actually used this well-known trick of the painter's trade. The Rouen images extend by implication well beyond the canvas, just catching a detail. The London paintings seem to have no edges. The horizontal lines of the bridges have no ends. The river is caught in a bubble.

Thus we see, in quite small canvases, Monet gradually moving towards his final masterpiece, a series with no beginning and no end, and no focus save for that point at which the spectator looks at any given moment.

Left: *Waterloo Bridge. Grey Day*
1903 Oil on canvas
65 × 100 cm ($25\frac{3}{5} \times 39\frac{2}{5}$ in)
National Gallery of Art, Washington D.C. Chester Dale Collection
The view of Waterloo Bridge from the Savoy shows the Shot Tower with factory and brewery chimneys over in Southwark. Looking east rather than west into the sun, there is a marked change in the light, as against the westward views of Charing Cross and Westminster, with rather more definition of the classical arched stone bridge.

Above: *Waterloo Bridge. Cloudy Weather*
1900 Oil on canvas
65 × 100 cm ($25\frac{3}{5} \times 39\frac{2}{5}$ in)
The Hugh Lane Municipal Gallery of Modern Art, Dublin
The bridge, crowded with traffic, stands dark and brooding over the fast-running Thames. Monet praised the London fog for eliminating details. When the weather changed with spring, he left London.

The Water-lilies

Secure and successful though it was, Monet's life was still heavy with misfortune on the eve of his undertaking the Water-lilies series. In 1908, his eyesight began to fail. He had suffered from chronic eyestrain and inflammation which had regularly interrupted his work, but now he was developing cataracts in both eyes. As well as blurred vision, all colours were now distorted by a reddish-brown cast, and Monet could no longer distinguish tints by looking at them, having to read the labels on the tubes to see what they were. However, he continued to work, refusing to be operated on in case the result might be even worse.

In spite of this severe handicap, he produced a remarkable series of paintings of the garden at Giverny, with its flower walks and borders, the lily pond with its Japanese bridge and wisteria, and the irises and yellow-gold willows. These pictures seemed to have remained in Monet's studio, for we have no comment on them by his contemporaries.

Just how much he could see and just how colour blind he had become are problematic. The only evidence in the work is a certain loose freedom, with vigorous brush work and very little overpainting. Paradoxically the canvases show none of the painful anxiety evident in the large Water-lilies project. In form and colour, these garden pictures remained unequalled until the self-conscious freedom of the 'Abstract Impressionists' of the mid-20th century.

The paint is dribbled, spattered and smeared. Liquid runs, thick impasto and acres of white or lightly stained canvas are left as they are, with no cleaning up, re-working or alteration. These works give meaning to that hackneyed phrase, 'a riot of colour': bright reds clash with vivid green, oranges and intense violet.

They are saved from descending into incoherence by Monet's masterly control over tone, painstakingly learned so many years before. His unerring eye for tone unmasked by colour enabled him to transcend the

limitations of colour blindness, and gave structure and order to work which, in detail, approaches the random. If a painter's eyesight is subject to encroaching restriction, then for as long as he can see at all, he paints from what he knows as much or even more than from what he sees. Thus, Monet's dissolving images are increasingly the result of intellectual effort, while they appear to be entirely instinctive.

In spite of the increasing demands being made upon Georges Clemenceau as a statesman (he was prime minister of France in 1906–9 and 1917–20), he always found time to visit Monet. The painter's morale was at a low ebb. Alice had died in 1911, and Monet was inconsolable. He stopped painting and even lost interest in the garden. Then, on the outbreak of the First World War, Jean Monet died at the age of 46 after a distressing illness. To rouse him from his depression, Clemenceau persuaded Monet to undertake a monumental project with the State as patron. Monet had often talked about a painting that would take him right back to the idea behind the canvases of the *Déjeuner* and *Women in the Garden*. This was to be a re-creation, in the round, of a landscape, a complete, endless diorama linking back on itself, full circle.

Left: *Water-lilies. The Japanese Bridge*
1918–24 Oil on canvas
89 x 116 cm (35 x 45$^{3}/_{5}$ in)
Minneapolis Society of Fine Arts, Minnesota
This magical picture is also tragic. Its astonishing colour and slashing brushstrokes are in no small part due to Monet's failing eyesight.

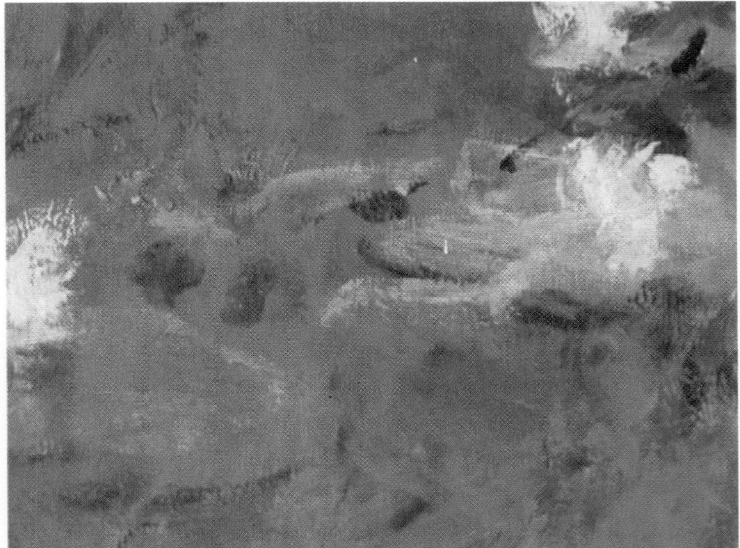

Opposite top: *Photograph of Monet and Clemenceau at Giverny*

Above: *Irises*
1916 – 26 Oil on canvas
200 x 149 cm (78¾ x 58⅝ in)
The National Gallery, London
Here Monet returned to matching form with brushwork.

The theme was to be Monet's lily pond at Giverny, and the series, for such it was, was given the general title of 'Water-lilies' (*Nymphéas*). It was by no means a new subject for Monet. In 1909, he had exhibited 48 lily pond studies which were hung in related groups to give a feeling of continuity beyond the picture frames. For the Water-lilies project, he needed a large oval gallery in which the long, horizontal canvases could be viewed with the minimum of interruption and with no angles between each picture. The Orangerie at the Louvre was reorganized to house the series.

Top and detail above:
Water-lilies. Morning
1916 – 26 Oil on canvas
197 x 1275 cm (77½ x 502 in)
Orangerie, Musée National du Louvre, Paris
By damming a stream and digging out a pond, Monet made his water garden with water-lilies, irises and weeping willows.

*In the Water-lily (*Nymphéas*) series, Monet's technique comes to culmination. Thin layers of paint are washed in, one over the other. Paint is dabbed and scumbled in tiny patches, or broadly imitates plant and leaf forms in thick vibrant colour.*

The paintings were to occupy Monet for the next ten years. It was a formidable undertaking for a man past middle age, suffering from double bereavement, with sons at the front, bad eyesight and a bronchial chest (Monet chain-smoked Caporals). He had a special studio built for the project: 12×23 m (39×75 ft), and 15m (49 ft) high. It was completed with difficulty, owing to the war-time shortage of materials and labour in 1916, but when it was, Monet was aghast at the monster he had created. Always energetically critical of the building taking place in Giverny and jealous of his view, he had, he felt, ruined his own house and garden with the ugliest building of them all.

Work progresses slowly on the large Water-lilies panels. On these, and on the studies for them, Monet painfully, anxiously worked and re-worked, scraping down, repainting and even destroying. He was conscious of the honour that had been bestowed on him and the responsibility that it carried, and felt that Clemenceau's reputation was also at stake.

Monet had become an increasingly private painter, ever more reluctant to show his work publicly. He painted to please himself, not self-indulgently for he was his own severest critic, but not primarily for public show. If the dealers and critics were pleased, then that was coincidental, for he did not paint with them in mind. His own standards had always been ahead of public taste and expectation. Now his works were not only to be subjected to public scrutiny, to be compared with those of the great Masters of the past, but they were meant to evoke a universal response, the equivalent of a public performance of music or drama.

Monet was constantly beset by doubts and crises of confidence, and his behaviour seemed calculated to provoke Clemenceau into cancelling the project. However, Clemenceau forbore Monet's truculence. The painter was finding it increasingly difficult to see, not just the subject, but the paintings themselves. He was tempted to destroy the panels and threatened to do so, while at the same time he was constantly in danger of inadvertently ruining them. The brilliant free garden studies may have been Monet's way of relieving the frustration that he had constantly felt with the Water-lilies.

Finally, in 1923, Monet underwent an operation for cataract, although, still distrustful of the outcome, he only agreed to have one eye operated upon. His sight

Water-lilies. The Two Willows (left part)
1916 – 26 Oil on canvas
197 × 1275 cm (77½ × 502 in)
Orangerie, Musée National du Louvre, Paris
The lily flowers and pads float on the surface of the water. Behind them the trees are reflected upside down. Behind the trees are reflected clouds and sky. Monet hardly ever drew in sketchbooks. The lily decorations were carved out from the flimsiest, tersest pencil notes, just a line here and there (see detail).

Water-lilies. Morning (left part of centre panel)
1916 – 26 Oil on canvas
Orangerie, Musée National du Louvre, Paris
Monet worked on these enormous panels under great difficulty. He followed old habits of repainting and altering, but on this scale he was simply unable to know whether he had finished or not. He was ageing, and no longer robust. The series remained in his studio until after his death in 1927.

Left: Photograph of Monet Working on Nymphéas

restored, at least in one eye, Monet was faced with further problems. He had to correct discrepancies between work done before and after the operation. Eventually the panels were completed, if that is the right word for work which, by definition, never could be finished.

The panels were not inaugurated and displayed in the Orangerie until 1927. Monet never saw them *in situ*. Finally unable to paint and prevented by age and ill health from constantly retouching the canvases, he still refused to be parted from them, and Clemenceau was content to wait for the end.

The Water-lilies have to be approached with that quiet expectation and a patient expenditure of time that one would bring to a performance in a concert hall. There is always a quiet hush in the gallery. The level of artificial light is low, and the eyes have to become accustomed. Slowly the eyes and brain begin to read shapes and colours in the panels. Gradually it dawns on us that the images are upside down. We are looking at the surface of the pond, in which sky, clouds and trees are reflected. Then images detach themselves from these reflections and float in front of them on the receding plane: green and blue lily pads crowned with white, pink, gold and blue lotus flowers. Some willow branches hang down in front of the picture plan. Questions arise: What is reflection, what is reality, when the whole thing is an illusion? Does the water have any local colour, or is it entirely violet sky and rosy cloud? There is no focal point, only our own centre of vision. At one moment, we are conscious of nothing but brush marks, the next, in the same view, they dissolve and vanish, and we are looking at a surface that we cannot grasp. We are gradually absorbed, surrounded.

With an effort of mind, we can analyse and appreciate the virtuosity of the painterly details. Thinly applied coats of paint build up into a bloom of misty blue, which is all depth and no surface. This is scarred and scratched. Thick blobs of impasto paint are apparently flung at the canvas, becoming light on water. The flowers are gashes of paint, floating above their thin reflections. All on top of a sky which appears above and behind us.

Visitors come into the room, stop and fall silent. Fidgeting dies away. Tourists walk round churches chattering to one another about what they see. Here, the still quiet of Monet's pond, not his studio, imposes itself.

Monet's Legacy

Monet died on 5 December, as 1926 drew to a close. He had outlived his contemporaries: Pissarro died in 1903, Cézanne in 1906, Rodin and Degas in 1917 and Durand-Ruel in 1922. Monet had continued into the age of the cinema, the phonograph, the aeroplane. Classical Cubism, with Picasso and Braque painting identical pictures, had gone through its first phase. The Futurists had published their manifesto and produced their symbolic paintings of speed and machines. Dadaism was under way. The Bauhaus was flourishing in Weimar, with Klee and Kandinsky teaching there. The Surrealists moved into Giverny and made it their village. Having been stunned by Stravinsky's *Rite of Spring*, audiences were being puzzled by Schoenberg. In the Soviet Union and in Holland, artists were producing purely abstract pictures in black and white and primary colours. Proust was writing *A la recherche du temps perdu*, modelling one of his characters upon Monet. Joyce was at work on *Finnegan's Wake*. The modern movement in architecture had produced its earliest monuments. Skirts had gone up, and their wearers cut their hair short and danced to jazz. It was another world, and Monet should have been an anachronism, a freak, a living dinosaur. The extraordinary thing is that his work leads not to an anticlimax, but to a culmination, a secular miracle.

Opposite: *The Seine at Giverny*
1897 Oil on canvas
81.6 × 100.3 cm (32 1/8 × 39 1/2 in)
National Gallery of Art, Washington D.C. Chester Dale Collection
Monet rose before dawn in order to be ready to catch the elusive early morning light. As the light changed and the sun rose through the mists, Monet worked away on one canvas after another.

Left: *Garden of the Artist at Giverny*
1900 Oil on canvas
81 × 92 cm (31 7/8 × 36 1/5 in)
Musée d'Orsay, Paris
Painted in the full light of day, Monet's pictures of his garden are brightly coloured and thickly painted, with strong accents of light and dark.

Overleaf: *Spring*
1886 Oil on canvas
65 × 81 cm (25 3/5 × 31 7/8 in)
Fitzwilliam Museum, Cambridge
Two of Monet's stepdaughters sit talking and reading on the grass. Simple in subject, but complex in technique, the white-pink blossom and blue of the sky seen through the leaves and branches are thick touches of paint placed side by side, and not superimposed.

During his visit to Norway in 1895, Monet had confessed to Henri Bang that he was chasing a dream:

'I want the unattainable. Other artists paint a bridge, a house, a boat and that's the end. They're finished. I want to paint the air that surrounds the bridge, the house, the boat, the beauty of the air in which these objects are located, and that is nothing short of impossible. If only I could satisfy myself with what is possible'.

The bridge, the house, the boat. Monet painted them all, and at times they were indistinguishable from the works of those artists who could be satisfied with the possible. But Monet deliberately made painting an impossible task. It was not simply a question of becoming a better painter, more skilled, more mature, experienced, selective, of finding his identity as an artist, of settling into his *métier*. As he progressed as a painter, his task became more, not less difficult. The closer he got to the ideal that he pursued, the more it eluded him. The self-imposed task became an obsession. To paint light, to paint with light, to attempt the impossible became a driving force that lasted as long as he did.

It accounts for the groups and series of paintings. If no single picture ever could achieve the ultimate objective, then by working on one painting after another, keeping them side by side, they might collectively get a little nearer than they could on their own, each dealing with one of the infinite facets of whatever subject was depicted. The subject, the end, was overtaken by the means. It merely became a medium, a peg to hang the objective on.

So Monet was to remain an experimenter, a traveller who could never arrive. Despite never achieving his end, the quest was not a failure. The result was a series of remarkable personal insights into paint, which open up to us an intense visual concentration. It puts us on a level with a force that we can appreciate and enjoy, while knowing that it remains forever beyond our grasp.

The story does not end with Monet. The Impressionists left more than a legacy of paintings now in galleries all over the world.

First, they opened the way for anyone to paint. Freed from the technicalities of the classical *atelier*, painting does not need elaborate preparation. Few will become artists, but many can paint for pleasure straight on to canvas. All amateurs show the influence of Impressionism, and so do many professionals.

Then there are the direct descendants of Impressionism. We can trace a succession from

Gauguin and Van Gogh to Expressionism, from Pointillism to pure Abstraction. Piet Mondrian left us a neat little autobiography in paint just to show how it was done. The late Monets painted at Giverny lead to *tachisme* and Abstract Impressionism, Jackson Pollock and modern American painting.

However, there is an even greater legacy than this, and one that is not so obvious. Without knowing the full significance of what they were doing, the Impressionists replaced the old tradition with a new one. Unfortunately, like all 'traditions', this new one can become just as cliché-ridden.

The Impressionists claimed the right of every artist to paint as he pleases. They set their own sights low, not foreseeing the extravagant excesses to which this right of freedom could lead. Patrons could make no claim; they would become 'collectors', bystanders who wait to see what will happen next. All significant art from now on would be outside the Establishment, the *Beaux Arts* schools and the Academies. Any artist joining the Establishment would be looked upon as a renegade, as selling out.

All significant art must be ahead of public expectation and public taste. Each artist in each generation must be different from his fellows, an experimenter whose work must be immediately recognizable as painted by 'so and so' – 'signed all over'. Above all, the critics are always wrong.

The contemporary critics, in Paris and London, made complete and utter fools of themselves over the Impressionists. Their mockery was returned a thousandfold. But there was a sense in which they were absolutely right. While disclaiming the epithet, the Impressionists really were unwitting revolutionaries who, without knowing what they were doing, opened the floodgates to the 20th century and all that is meant by the term 'Modern Art', good and bad. After them, it was every man for himself.

INDEX

Page numbers in italics refer to illustrations

Photographic acknowledgments
Aberdeen Art Gallery and Museums 96–97; Art Institute of Chicago 22, 67 top; Ashmolean Museum, Oxford 24–25; Barber Institute of Fine Arts, The University of Birmingham 52–53, 87 top; Bayerische Staatsgemäldesammlungen, Munich 62 top; Bridgeman Art Library, London 10 bottom, 32, 56–57, 88–89, 90–91, 92–93, 112 bottom; Sterling and Francine Clark Art Institute, Williamstown, Massachusetts 11, 82, 102–103; Courtauld Institute Galleries, London 49 top, 61, 75; Mary Evans Picture Library, London 81; Fitzwilliam Museum, Cambridge 98, 118; Giraudon, Paris 6–7, 9, 12–13, 15, 28 bottom, 30, 35, 36, 38, 46 top, 50, 50–51, 58 bottom, 62–63, 64–65, 67 bottom, 70–71, 73; 74, 80, 102, 106–107, 109, 113 top, 114, 115, 117; Glasgow Art Gallery and Museum 77; Richard Green, London 22–23, 26–27; Kuntshalle Bremen 37; Hugh Lane Municipal Gallery of Modern Art, Dublin 111; Mansell Collection, London 14 top, 28 top left, 66 top, 87 bottom, 106 left, 106 right; Museum of Fine Arts Boston, Massachusetts 58 top; National Gallery, London (reproduced by courtesy of the Trustees) 18 top, 28 top right, 39 top, 40–41, 42, 46 bottom, 46–47, 48–49, 68–69, 72, 82–83, 113 bottom left; National Gallery of Scotland, Edinburgh 94–95, 100–101; National Museums and Galleries on Merseyside, Walker Art Gallery, Liverpool 20–21; Novosti Press Agency, London 29; Philadelphia Museum of Art, Pennsylvania 33; Sammlung Oskar Reinhart "Am Römerholz", Winterthur 43, 78–79; Roger-Viollet, Paris 10 top, 25 top, 25 bottom, 86, 112 top, 114–115; Tate Gallery, London 84–85; Victoria and Albert Museum, London 39 bottom, 49 bottom; Wadsworth Atheneum, Hartford, Connecticut 62 bottom; John Webb, Cheam 99.

Front cover:	(top) *Poppies.* 1873. Musée d'Orsay, Paris (bottom left) *Le bassin aux nympheas: harmonie rose.* 1900. Musée d'Orsay, Paris (bottom right) *Grain Stacks. End of summer. Morning.* Musée d'Orsay, Paris (all photographs Bridgeman Art Gallery)
Back cover:	*Poplars on the Epte.* 1891. National Gallery of Scotland, Edinburgh
Titlespread:	*The bridge at Argenteuil.* 1874. National Gallery of Art, Washington D.C. Collection of Mr. and Mrs. Paul Mellon
Contents spread:	*Woman seated under the willows.* 1880. National Gallery of Art, Washington D.C. Chester Dale Collection.

Diagrams by Bernard Myers